Racial Profiling Disorder
Hate Groups and Domestic Terrorism

Racial Profiling Disorder
Hate Groups and Domestic Terrorism

by Dr. Demetrius Edwin Ford Ph. D. J.D., Psy.D.

Senior Publisher
Steven Lawrence Hill Sr

A Publisher Trademark Title page

ASA Publishing Corporation
An Accredited Publishing House with the BBB
www.asapublishingcorporation.com

The Landmark Building
23 E. Front St., Suite 103, Monroe, Michigan 48161

All Rights Reserved. No part of this publication may be reproduced, stored in a retrieval system or transmitted in any form or by any means electronic, mechanical, photocopying, recording or otherwise, without the prior written permission of the publisher. Author/writer rights to "Freedom of Speech" protected by and with the "1st Amendment" of the Constitution of the United States of America. This is a work of non-fiction; Educational Learning in Socialism in relation to Racial Profiling. Any resemblance to actual events, locales, person living or deceased that is not related to the author's literacy is entirely coincidental.

With this title/copyrights page, the reader is notified that the publisher does not assume, and expressly disclaims any obligation to the authors own workings, within the author's rights as manuscript owner. Nor is the publisher obligated to obtain and/or include any other information other than that provided by the author (unless permitted) and within the ownership rights thereof. Any belief system, promotional motivations, including but not limited to the use of non-fictional/fictional characters and/or characteristics of this book, are within the boundaries of the author's own creativity in order to reflect the nature and concept of the book.

Any and all vending sales and distribution not permitted without full book cover and this copyrights page.

Copyrights©2017 Dr. Demetrius Edwin Ford, All Rights Reserved
Book Title: Racial Profiling Disorder *Hate Groups and Domestic Terrorism*
Date Published: 08.29.2017 / Edition 1 *Trade Paperback*
Book ID: ASAPCID2380724
ISBN: 978-1-946746-17-7
Library of Congress Cataloging-in-Publication Data

This book was published in the United States of America.
Great State of Michigan

A Publisher Trademark Copyrights page

Racial Profiling Disorder
Hate Groups and Domestic Terrorism

by Dr. Demetrius Edwin Ford Ph. D. J.D., Psy.D.

Foreword

What did Vice President Joe Biden mean by his statement "they wanna put y'all back in chains." I've not had the opportunity to ask him and it would be politically incorrect for him to elaborate, considering the fact that he's the Vice President and could be running for President in 2016. After being criticized for being gaff prone, Joe Biden didn't deny being gaff prone but responded that he never said anything that he didn't mean. Now I've heard many statements concerning the philosophical and psychological motivation of many racist White Institutions, but none explained it better than Joe Biden's statement. The 13th Amendment freed Blacks from slavery and abolished involuntary servitude. However, today's slavery is seen in racial profiling that ends with loss of life, liberty and the pursuit of happiness for Blacks. Racial profiling is the focus of this book. It is passive aggressive-covert racism. But this book uncovers it and provides insight into those who perpetrate racial profiling through camouflage and institutional racism. While ISIS the primary terrorism threat to the world, WHITESIS is the primary domestic terror threat to Black American. Formal lynchings ended in 1968, but legal police lynchings took its place, under the color of law. Lastly, Trayvon Martin, Michael Brown, Tamir Rice, Eric Gardner and others were not just lynched by single police officers or neighborhood watchmen, but they were racially profiled and lynched by the institutions in American that promote, encourage and allow for such lynching to occur.

Abstract

In my opinion, Racial Profiling is a disorder that should be considered by the American Psychiatric Association, Diagnostic and Statistical Manual, committee. This syndrome is the result of research I conducted that's described in this book. Racial Profiling Disorder should be de- fined as (1) hatred, implicit or explicit for others from ethnic-minority populations (2) obsessive thoughts of ways to demonize, degrade or discredit individuals from minority populations (3) compulsive hostility, rage, disgust anger and animosity toward members from minority population (4) efforts to intellectualize, justify, rationalize, or politicize their views (5) clinically significant distress or hostility or impairment in social, occupational or other important areas (6) is not the results of other medical illnesses or substance use. RPD is the foundation of Institutional racism which is so-pervasive today that institutions have persuaded the FBI to remove from its website links to the Southern Poverty Law Center and the Anti-defamation League. The Southern Poverty Law Center and Anti-defamation League have historically worked with the FBI on identifying and tracking hate groups.

Hate Groups: racial profilers implicitly participant in underground hate groups because their efforts are consistent, pervasive and strategic at demeaning, marginalizing and being hostile towards minorities. The Southern Poverty Law Center among others, define and track hate groups as "beliefs and practices that attack or malign an entire class of people (SPLC, 2013). As of 2012 there were about 1012 hate groups in the United States including 196, neo-Nazi group, 186 separate KKK groups, 113 Black Separatist groups, 111 White Nationalist groups, 98 White Power Skinhead groups, 93 neo-Confederate groups 39 Christian Identity groups and 90 General Hate groups (anti-gay, Holocaust denial, racist music, radical traditionalist Catholic and others) SPLC, 2013.

The connection between Racial Profiling Disorder and Hate Groups is that Hate Groups encourages and brainwashes individuals into development RPD. Likewise, when one with Racial Profiling Disorder feels challenged by his/her beliefs, the Racial Profiler will find comfort in Hate Groups which will further validate the Racial Profiler's ideas.

Domestic Terrorism. The FBI describes domestic terror as "the unlawful use of force or violence, committed by a group of two or more individuals, against persons or property to intimidate or coerce a government, the civilian population, or any segment thereof, in furtherance of political or social objectives. The Patriot Act also defines domestic terrorism. A few groups on the domestic terror, FBI list are the KKK, Sovereign Citizens United, Aryan Nation, Army of God, Black Liberation Army, The Covenant, The Sword, and the Arm of the Lord, The Jewish Defamation League, Phineas Priesthood, etc. A Some attacks from the above consists of the Oklahoma City Bombing, the Wall Street Bombing, The Unabomber attacks, the Wisconsin Sikh Temple Shooting (James, 2009, FBI, 2014). Domestic terror is that result of the racial profiler's aim to oppresses, kill, steal and destroy the target group or person. This can be seen in the Police brutality and shootings of unarmed Black males. Blacks have been under assault, since Blacks were forcefully migrated from Africa to the America. While some are obsessed with foreign terror, Domestic Terror is ever present in America. The increasing number of Hate Groups are at an all-time high. Hate is equivalent to murder (1 John 3:15, Bible). Racial Profiling cases are increasing exponentially. There is an obsession with foreign terror by many in America but in- difference towards Black who are terrorized and killed weekly by hate groups including some police in America. The demonization and in- difference toward Blacks is seen in the way President Obama is treat- ed. The hate, racial profiling and domestic terror that President Obama endures daily from hate news outlets, congresspersons and right wing radical is unprecedented. This hate serves as propaganda for international terror groups. The love for America is called into question when hate groups and racists attack the leader of America, the President. If one loves America, on would also love the leader of America, even if one has differences with the President.

Acts implicit or explicit of individuals with RPD, Hate Groups and Domestic Terrorists all have the following in common. They oppose in- creasing the minimum wage, they oppose Obama's Immigration Bill, and they oppose Affirmative Action which has been diluted by the U.S. Supreme Court. They never saw a police shooting that wasn't justified. They implicitly believe that Black are criminals. They oppose Civil Rights and Black history in general. The oppose sections 4 and 5 of the 15th Amendment that was stuck down by the U.S. Supreme Court. Finally, they oppose Obama Care or the Affordable Care Act.

When the young rich ruler came to Jesus he said "good master, what must I do to have eternal life?" The rich ruler first tried to puff Jesus up, so that Jesus would lift him up. But Jesus replied, "There is none good but the father, which art in heaven." Jesus then told him to keep the commandments. The rich young ruler said he did from his youth up. Keeping the commandments meant keeping the Law. Many right- wing radicals and conservative today use Christianity because they feel they have been faithful in obeying the Bible. But Jesus threw a monkey wrench into the rich young ruler plans. Jesus equated treatment or the poor, as a commandment too. This commandment, the rich young rulers, and conservative today fail at. Jesus then said "take all you have, sell it and give it to the poor, then you shall have treasure in heaven (Matt. 19:16-22)." The rich young ruler loved his wealth so- much that he rejected Jesus' offer and went away in sorry. A person with RPD, hate and who terrorizes marginalizes and demonizes Blacks and the poor to be criminal may learn a great lesson from the rich young ruler.

Table of Contents

Ferguson 9

Chapter 1
  High Tech Lynching 29

Chapter II
  The Pathological Development of Racial Profiling in America 39

Chapter III
  How to Detect Racial Profiling 85

Chapter IV
  Hand's Up: Real Life Experience of Racial Profiling 95

Chapter V
  Guns Down: Conclusions 133

References 149

Ferguson

Hands–up is the new a term for Racial Profiling of Black men by the police. Hands-up, is a term that is being used to break down walls of institutional racism involving the (police, schools, government, banking, housing, voting, employment, religion, etc.). Hands-up is a manifestation of racial profiling where one fears death or serious body injury, as a result of being stereotyped. In this book, I investigated experiences of 12 Black men who were victims of racial profiling. I then interpreted their experience from an interdisciplinary perspective. This book serves, as a good lesson on diversity, inclusion, understanding multiculturalism and in placing one's faith into practice of civility and humanity. In this book the reader will see how it's one thing to understand the law, multiculturalism, psychology, and humanistic philosophies from a cognitive-cerebral perspective, like attending a workshop, but it's more than a notion to actually put those oaths to be peace officers, lawyers, judges, teachers, doctors, and other professionals into practice of protecting those we severe constitutional rights to life, liberty and their pursuits of happiness.

Michael Brown's friend, Dorian Johnson who was with Michael Brown at the time of the shooting explained that Officer Wilson accosted them and told them "get the f_ _k out of the street then pulled off, then tried to reverse and before they could move he tried to jump out of his car. Because he was too-close to them, the car door bounced off Brown and Johnson. Officer Wilson then grabbed Brown by the neck. There was a tug of war and Wilson threatened to shoot Brown and did fire his gun, hitting Brown. Brown and Johnson then ran. Johnson hid by a vehicle while Officer Wilson exited his vehicle and pursed Brown. Officer Johnson fired once and Brown turned around with his hands-up. Wilson then fired multiple shots and Brown fell to the ground. After a prolonged time, Officer Wilson refused to write a police report and the Prosecutor refused to Charge Officer Wilson. During these proceedings, one of the assistant prosecutors erroneously provided a 1979 law that allowed police to shoot fleeing felons. That law had been overturned in 1985 by the U.S. Supreme Court. Subsequently, the Grand jury after a historic tenure, incredibly refused to indict Officer Wilson on any charges.

Furthermore, a female witness said that Officer Wilson was talking with Michael Brown through the window of his patrol car, and then Officer Wilson grabbed Brown. There was a scuffle, and then two shots were fired. Brown ran away from Wilson to where she was standing, near a telephone pole. She indicated that Brown stopped running, his arms went up and he turned around, and walked back towards the police, saying "I give up." She said that Officer Wilson then got out of the police car and fired at least four more times until Brown, who was unarmed, collapsed to the ground. Wilson fired a total of 12 shots (Hunter, Huffington Post 11/25/14). Another man who witnessed the incident while on his porch claimed that Brown was shot in the back while he was running away. According to his testimony, Brown then turned around, put up his hands, and said, "Don't shoot." In my opinion, just because there was no bullet entry to the back, doesn't mean that Officer Wilson didn't shoot at Brown, as Brown ran away. While there are conflicts between witnesses - there are issues of fact that raise enough probable cause for at least an indictment on involuntary manslaughter, and the case should have gone to trial. The trickery of a biased criminal justice institution who mis-instruct or fail to instruct juries, often prevent Black families, like the Brown family from having their day in court. Weeks later when grand jury results and witness statements were released, Prosecutor, Robert McCullough, left out Johnson's testimony and later apologized when he was caught red-handed, promising to make the available, as soon as possible. As Al Sharpton often says "Gotch ya." Hands up represent the disproportionate number of unarmed Black males being killed by the Police. Hands-up does not necessarily mean that a Black male is innocent of all crimes; it just means that he's innocent of death and brutality at the hands of the police. No person is innocent of all things. Even President Nixon said "I ain't no crook." We'll, he was a crook but not worthy of death that unarmed Black males are getting at the hands of trigger happy police. Michael Brown was guilty of a misdemeanor, petty theft, not strong man robbery that extremist try to demonize him with. And like Nixon, Michael Brown was not worthy of murder by the police.

What's also troubling is the efforts of right wing extremist to cherry-pick the Justice Department Ferguson report in futile attempts to justify Officer Wilson and discredit the Hand's Up narrative. Seriously! Do these civil right opponents, think their crooked, psychobabble gibberish will fly? First of all, when did right wing extremist start praising General Holder? Like President Obama, the last I heard, extremist were calling Mr. Holder a terrorist and race baiter. Now he's the savior. I'd like to see extremist praise Eric Holder for the second investigation of his complete report. Some of its findings are below.

There was not prosecutorial evidence to charge Officer Wilson. This does not mean that there wasn't significant evidence or even evidence sufficient to prove that Officer Wilson was responsible for the Death of Michael Brown in civil court. This just means that there was not enough evidence to hold him responsible under the criminal statutes. However, complaints are being filed, as we speak that will seek to hold him responsible under the civil statutes. The civil statutes burden of proof is much lower, only 51% and opposed to about 95% under the criminal statutes. So Officer Wilson and extremists should not count their chickens before they hatch. If Officer Wilson loses the civil trial, then he will be judged to be responsible for the death of Michael Brown and will pay a hefty price.

In my opinion, the only reason that Officer Wilson was not charged, indicted and therefore found guilty in a criminal trial was because of structured, institutional racism within the Ferguson criminal justice system (as was discovered in the 2nd investigation by the DOJ). There were 7 racial barriers to Officer Wilson's criminal indictment. (1) The Ferguson Police Department and Prosecutor McCulloch let Officer Wilson get away without immediately, writing a report; this allowed Officer Wilson to cater his story to the exculpatory direction of the ballistic evidence. (2) Prosecutor McCulloch refused to invite and independent investigator: this would have allowed for objective discovery of evidence. By the time the FBI & U.S. Attorney's Office got involved, evidence certainly could have been lost or manipulated to favor Officer Wilson. An Independent Investigator is recommendation by the Justice Department in all police shooting cases. (3) Prosecutor McCulloch failed to appoint an Independent Prosecutor. This prevented a new objective prosecutor to come in and charge Officer Wilson, allowing McCulloch to like the Wizard of Oz to be Judge, Jury and Executioner. Appointing an Independent Prosecutor is another recommendation made by the Justice Department in all police shooting cases. (4) Prosecutor McCulloch refused to charge Officer Wilson. There were about 16 witnesses who said that Michael Brown's hands were up including his associated Dorian Johnson. But Officer Wilson could have been charged with 2 counts of attempted murder for trying to run over Brown and Johnson; he could have been charged with 2 counts of felonious assault for hitting them with his door; he could have been charges with 1 count of aggravated assault for choking Brown; he could have been charged with 1 count of attempted murder for his initial shooting of Brown and he could have been charged with premeditated murder for killing Brown.

In essence the issues of hands-up not only go to the premeditated murder charge. There should have been 6 other charges outside of murder. Dorian Johnson was a Res Gestate Witness and only one witness is sufficient evidence to recommend a warrant and a preliminary hearing.

Then trained Attorneys could cross examine all evidence, find the truth and a diverse jury/fact finder could decide if there is sufficient evidence to warrant the charges. (5) Prosecutor McCulloch request for a Grand Jury would allow him to advocate for the Dorian Wilson, the Defendant, instead the People and the victim Michael Brown. (6) During the Grand Jury, Assistant Prosecutor Alizadeh gave the jurors an outdated 1979 law stating that the police could shoot a fleeing felon, when in fact in 1985, the U.S. Supreme Court overturned that very law. She must have known this, being an experienced, senior assistant prosecutor. Naturally this confused the jury. And when a juror asked about the Supremacy clause, whether a Federal law trumps state law, the juror was told, not to worry about that. (7) Assistant Prosecutor Alizadeh was racist; right in the middle of Dorian Johnson's testimony of the shooting of Michael Brown as Michael Brown was running, Assistant Prosecutor Alizadeh makes stereotypical racist responses, regarding sagging pants. It seemed that the Assistant Prosecutor who should have been advocating for the victim, Michael Johnson was actually trying to demonize him. Q What is Big Mike doing? A At that time Big Mike's hands was up, but not so much up in the air because he had been struck already in this region somewhere on this. It was like this hands is up and this hand is kind of like down sort of. A His hands were nowhere near his waist? No, his hands never went down towards his waistline or anything, like he didn't have a belt on or anything. Q Was he sagging, was his pants sagging or you say he wasn't wearing a belt? A Yeah, at that time he didn't look like he was sagging. Q That's okay if he was, I'm trying to get the picture. A At that time I wasn't looking for, I was looking more at him and the officer because how he stopped, I felt like he was shot again, so now I'm really fearing like, wow, he's been shot twice. Not knowing for sure he has been shot twice, definitely know he has been shot one. Q

Okay. The reason why I am asking you about the sagging, we probably all know the kind of, you know, how young folks do it. A Yeah. Q A lot of times when they are sagging, their pants are down so low that you can actually see the waist area. Q Right. That's what I'm asking, was he sagging or do you recall? A No. Q Was not, but no belt? A No belt on. Q Did he have a weapon that day? A No, ma'am. Q Did you? A No, ma' am, none whatsoever, anything like that" (State of Missouri v. Daren Wilson, Dorian Johnson's Grand Jury Testimony, September 10, 2014). By the way the word sagging spelled backwards is NIGGAS.

Another contributor to injustice in the Michael Brown case is eyewitness testimony. I believe that the people who claimed that Michael Brown's hands were never-up had problems recollecting or identifying the facts of what they saw. Remember in the Trayvon Martin Killing, a witness said that Trayvon was on top of Zimmerman with a dark hoodie. Another witness said someone was on top with a white shirt. In the D.C. Sniper case, a witness said that the killer was driving a van, but it turned out to be a 4 door sedan. In the Oklahoma bombing case, a witness said that there were two perpetrator at the scene, but there was only one. Most wrongful conviction cases are overturned because of problems with eyewitness testimonies. Therefore, in cases like the Michael Brown case, where there are conflicts between witnesses, there must be cross examinations by attorneys from both sides, then the case should go to a jury. Now let me get back to the Department of Justice Report on Ferguson. While this report did not criminally indict Officer Wilson, due to historical racism laced in the federal laws, this report does not exonerate Officer Wilson of civil responsibility for the Death Michael Brown. While I think Eric Holder is the greatest U.S. Attorney General in the History of this country and has done more for Blacks and Justice for everyone, than all previous U.S. Attorney generals combined, Mr. Holder is not perfect, and I believe he made some mistake in the Ferguson race crises. First of all, I believe the Mr. Holder, was too-late in investigating the Ferguson incident. Officer Wilson, like Martin Zimmerman, the Travon Martin killer was allowed to walk away with evidence. Holder relied on the Ferguson Prosecutor to do the right thing and waited too late; much evidence could have been loss and the fix was already in.

Hypnotrickology had kicked in and many officials in Ferguson were sleeping in the same bed in efforts to protect Michael Brown, maintain their revenue, and keep their jobs. It is almost impossible to indict police officers for killing Black males in America. Eric Gardner was choked to death in broad daylight, no indictment. Tamir Rice was shot in two seconds, no indictment yet. Trayvon Martin was hunted by a neighborhood watchman police, no conviction. Shawn Crawford was killed by police in Walmart for examine a BB gun, no indictment. The list goes on. So the sad reality is that American's Justice system gives the police the license to kill Black males. But should this be such a big surprise. Traditionally, in this country, Blacks had no rights or justice and slave or free, could not be American citizens (Dread Scott v. Sanford, 1799). Furthermore, let's not forget that Ferguson is the state of the Missouri Compromise of 1820 that regulated slavery in the western territories and maintained slavery South of the 36/30 parallel. In essence Ferguson is a classic example of structured institutional racism.

I give Mr. Holder credit. He knew that some the federal civil rights, criminal laws are just decoration. The proofs within the Federal Civil Right Laws make it almost impossible to indict White police defendants. Holder is working to address that problem before he leaves office. Holder used the Federal civil, desperate-impact statutes to evaluate and condemn the city of Ferguson with implicit and explicit racism.. I think Holder is well aware that there is a movement afoot in this country to attack all civil right initiatives and put Blacks back in chains, as Vice President Biden stated. Affirmative Action has been diluted where the U.S. Supreme Court ruled that States can regulate race based Affirmative Action in college admission.

Many extremists criticized Michael Brown's father for expressing shock and disbelief and demanding that Ferguson be burned down. Well based on the DOJ's report it looks like he's getting his wish. The Police Chief resigned, the City Manager resigned, a Judge resigned, police officers have been fired. Court workers have resigned. But most importantly, Officer Wilson is no longer licensed to kill; he's like Cain in the Bible who killed Abel, a Vagabond.

The DOJ report indicated that 0 Whites and 35 Blacks received 5 or more citations at a time; Blacks are 26 percent less likely to carry contraband but 50 percent more likely to be stopped by the police; Backs are on 67 percent of the population but 85 percent of the traffic stops in Ferguson. Blacks receive 90 percent of police-tasers, 90 percent of the "manner of walking along the road way offenses." Blacks are 93 percent of the victims of excessive force and 100 percent of police dog bites. The DOJ reported that Ferguson used law enforcement to collect revenue instead of protecting the public. There were multiple constitutional violations by law enforcement officials. There were unreasonable searches and seizures (classic racial profiling) and excessive force. The police created a toxic environment. At every level of law enforcement this racism was seen. Ferguson collected 50% more revenue in 2014 than in 2010 that was not driven by increased crime. Taxes and other revenue tricks collected 1.3 million in fines and fees. Ticket revenue is expected to exceed 3 million in 2015, doubling that in the previous five years. Again, the police served as a collection agency for the courts instead of a law enforce men agency. Multiple charges were made for a single conduct. Some offers competed to see who could issues the most tickets, one issued 14 tickets in a single stop. In 2007 a woman received a parking ticket for $152. She paid over $500 was arrested twice and spent 6 days in jail; yet and still owed over $500. The DOJ's report indicated that there were dozens of similar stories. Ferguson resident's 1st Amendment constitutions rights were infringed upon. Residents couldn't express themselves and couldn't record. Their 4th Amendment constitutional rights were also violated as they were stopped without reasonable suspicion and without probable cause. A Black man who was sitting in his car resting after playing basketball was accosted by a police officer, accused of being a pedophile and told to get out of his car. When the man refused, the police officer pulled out his gun and pointed it at the man. He was arrested, charged with 8 counts and lost his job. The report further indicated that there was no alternative explanation as to the disproportionate treatment of Blacks in Ferguson other than implicit and explicit racism. Finally, the reported explained that immediate action not mere discussions were needed to address the problem (DOJ, 2015 Ferguson).

"Rome like the U.S. was the leading world military power in during the first Century. Rome was not defeated by a foreign nation but was later destroyed by its internal sins. America is similar to Rome. Many are in denial of racism like an alcoholic are to their addictions and would rather deal with anything but race, however, I believe that the greatest threat to America is not Iran, North Korea, Russia, Alkeda nor ISIS but WHITESIS. What I mean by WHITESIS is domestic terrorism, perpetrated by racist police officers and White institutions against Blacks. This study is not an indictment on non-racist White police officers, or non-racist White people, but those who, as Joe Biden put it want to put Blacks back in chains (explicitly or implicitly). The primary manifestation of racism today is in the form of Racial Profiling, which is a type of institutional racism. This is why I studied this topic because I see it as the single more important threat to America and the single most important cause of Black poverty and Black crime in America. Martin Luther King Jr. (quoting Victor Hugo) said that a soul left in darkness will sin, but the guilty on is not he who sin, but he who causes the darkness. Famous Positive Psychologist Martin Seligman's research demonstrated how trauma caused learned helplessness. Blacks have undergone racial trauma in America for 395 years. This trauma was so severe in its climax that Slavery almost destroyed America during the Civil War. Today there's a reversal of racial progress. All of the police shootings in America today are not anomalies but normalcies. How did America get here?

Abuse of the Bible and misinterpretations relative to their God given right to oppress Blacks is central to Blacks being racially profiled and forcefully migrated to America from Africa into slavery. This practice has largely been based on Whites rationalizing why Blacks should be slaves. Whites even used the Bible where it states servant obey your masters (Colossians 3:22) to justify slavery. It's interesting how Whites used the Bible to justify slavery, but conveniently forgot that Jesus said ". . . the greatest among you must be your servant" (Matthew 23:11). Therefore, If White slave-master-chiefs did not want to be slaves; this logic compels Whites to not to have slaves Some Whites misinterpret (Genesis 9:25) in the Old Testament of the Bible, as a curse to all Black people to justify Black enslavement. But Noah, cursed only one of his grandchildren, Canaan. This was not a curse to the entire descendants of Ham in perpetuity. In addition, the New Testament would abolish any curse, through Christ. But more specifically, Noah s said that only Canaan was cursed. The Bible says "curse be Canaan and . . . he shall be a servant of Shem" (Genesis 9:25-16). Canaanites are not necessarily Africans; some are Semitic, some Africans. Canaan is the father of the Sidon (Coogan, 2009). Ham had many descendants including but not exclusive to Blacks, but including Indians and Mongloids.

Statistical Racism is the primary strategy that is used today to demonize and racially profile Blacks, as being criminal. Certain individual and institutions would like America to think that Blacks commit more crimes than Whites. They would cite statistics used from various sources, mostly the FBI to make biased conclusions. Extremist need Blacks to be more criminal in order to justify slavery and to maintain support for institutional racism and the prison industrial complex. Moreover, many believe that Blacks are more violent than Whites in order to justify having a racist personality and to alleviate their guilt and pressures to change.

People who believe that Blacks are more criminal than Whites are misinterpreting statistics by seeing an effect that is not present. In Science, this is what is called a Type I Error; it is when the null-hypothesis is rejected, even though it is true. The null hypothesis here is that Blacks are not more criminal than Whites. The argument that Blacks are more criminal than Whites is based on FBI crime data but erroneous conclusions that Blacks are about 6 times more like to commit homicides than Whites. The truth is that there is a diminutive number of Blacks who are actually more likely to commit homicides than Whites. Making this type of error is a litmus test for detecting racism. For instance, it is an error to say that Muslims killed Americans by destroying the World Trade Center buildings because Muslims did not. If Muslims destroyed the World Trade Center buildings then 1.6 billion Muslims would have descended on New York and blew-up the World Trade Center buildings. This is the same Type I Error that Bill O'Riley made stating "Muslims killed us" while he was a guess on the View. Whoopee Goldberg and Joy Behar were so offended and outraged that they walked-out on live television. But equally appalling was the fact that other hosts on the view were so immune to racism and Xenophobic statements that they didn't even realize that a racist attack even occurred.

The Federal Bureau of Investigations, Uniform Crime Reports for 2012 indicated that there were 8,506 homicides; Blacks were responsible for 4,203 and Whites were responsible for 4,101. First of all, statistically there is no significant difference between these homicides. Since there is no statistical difference, racist compare rates between Black and White population and come up with Blacks being about 6 times more likely to commit homicide than whites. Even with this result, what Whites are really measuring is Black poverty which is a product of implicit oppression by White Institutions.

I believe that Whites are substantially less likely to be charged, convicted and sentenced for crimes. Contrary to the popular saying that Justice is Blind. In America, Justice is White and sometimes green. Let's test my hypothesis, if I were a betting man, I would bet that there will be zero prosecutions for what is called Enhanced Interrogation Techniques (torture) and no perpetrators will be listed in the FBI, Uniform Crime Reports. On the other hand, when Blacks terrorize people, it's simply called-crimes that will certainly be published in the FBI, Uniform Crime Reports. Moreover, Blacks receive felonies in order to eliminate them from the workforce. When this happens, Black males have no recourse but to commit additional crimes to survive and return to the prison plantations where White institutions bill $50,000 per year, per inmate.

Instead of using scientific racism, in order to truly determine how likely Blacks are to commit homicides, the proper test is to ask what percent of the Black population committed the 4,203 homicides in 2012. This equation is simply completed by dividing 4203 by 40 million and multiplying it by 100. When this is done, the statistical result of the percentage of the Black population who committed crimes in 2012 is zero. The true statistical answer is 0.011 % or one hundredth of a percent which is statistically 0. But racist need to prove that Blacks are violent so they can spin the propaganda at the expense of Black males being lynched by racist police who think Blacks are all murderers. When conservative taking heads amp up the rhetoric about Blacks being criminal, they in fact create and encourage violence and police hostility, towards Blacks. According to the FBI, Uniform Crime Reports of the 27 different types of criminal offenses reported, Whites had higher criminal offenses than Blacks in 25 categories. Blacks only had higher crime offenses in 2 categories. This is shocking information-isn't it!

Blacks are not more criminal than Whites. If Whites are profiled, charged, prosecuted, convicted and sentenced at the equitable rate of Blacks, crime statistics would not show Blacks having a higher rate of crime. Psychologist Martin Seligman addressed the effects of trauma on dogs being shocked. For Blacks, I call this Racial Shock Trauma resulting in a learned helplessness manifested in disbelief in the American Dream and living the nightmare of the street-life, as second class citizens. Therefore, racism deprives Blacks of employment, living wages, creates trauma, and causes crime in the Black community. In this, Black young men give-up just like Seligman dogs gave up after being repeatedly shocked in their efforts to be free from the shock traumatize. So when the American dream is snatched from Black males, the only thing left is street employment (selling drugs, joining gangs, robbing and stealing, etc.). Black men are victim of American injustice. But as seen in slavery, the South benefited financially from the trauma and enslavement of Blacks. Today all of America benefits from the enslavement of Black males. The prison industrial complex is a multi-billion dollar industry, not including the police, prosecutors, courts, and other institutions in America that benefit directly or indirectly from the racial profiling and oppression of Black males.

U.S. Chief Justice Warren in the 1954 Brown v. Board of Education case held that the vestiges of slavery have left Blacks with a badge of inferiority that is likely to never be undone. The court then concluded that separate is inherently unequal. It is the separate discriminatory treatment of Blacks, the racial profiling, the employment and income inequality that are the cause-in-fact of the problems in the Black community-not that Black men more criminal than Whites. As Martin Luther King Jr. said Black American has been given a bad check that has returned non-sufficient funds.

There are several studies that show that Jails are built for Blacks and not Whites. The zero tolerance programs prosecute and execute Blacks, while giving Whites a Pass. In the Tamir Rice and Sean Crawford cases, there was zero tolerance before the police shootings. Once the police heard the words Black and Gun, they're mentality became shoot first, then ask questions. President Obama and the U. S. Attorney General, Eric Holder, denounced Zero Tolerance programs in School because research discovered that while White children gets passes, Black children get prosecuted. Blacks are disproportionately racially profiled, charged, prosecuted, convicted and sentenced to much longer sentences than

Whites. In the 1980's until 2010 Blacks were prosecuted and a rate of 100:1 relative to crack/cocaine use; the change is now 18:1, without any evidence that crack users are likely to be more violent. It should be 1:1.

It is important to understand that in almost every case of a police shooting, the killing is rarely recorded, as a homicide and the police are rarely convicted. These results do not factor in to the FBI statistical crime reports of White Homicides. Historically, the phenomenon of Whites being convicted of lynching or murdering Blacks have rarely been included in crime reports because historically Whites either were either not prosecuted or got off after being prosecuted. A good example of the police getting away with murdering Blacks was seen in Hurricane Katrina.

Hurricane Katrina occurred in 2005. Due to the slow government response, several New Orleans residents experienced severe hunger and thirst and without resources some went into various stores and took food and water. They were demonized as hoodlums. Police made several false reports of crimes that did not occur. Over 40,000 troops were sent to Louisiana-as if it was a war. In one incident on the Dazinger Bridge. A Police Officer lied about an officer being down. Two Black men (17-year-old James Brissette and 40-year-old Ronald Madison) were shot and killed by the police. In 2010 a federal jury convicted several officers of multiple offenses including a cover-up. Yet, some convictions were vacated in 2013, due to prosecutorial misconduct. Again, some police officers commit crimes but rarely are successfully prosecuted. In essence, institutional racism has a way of protecting the ones it wants to protect and convicting and incarcerating Black men.

Even the bombing of 16th street Baptist Church resulted in no homicide convictions until about 25 years later. In 1963 several KKK were charged with murdering Addie Mae Collins (age 14), Denise McNair (age 11), Carole Robertson (age 14), and Cynthia Wesley (age 14), who attended Sunday School at 16th Street Baptist Church in Birmingham, Alabama. Robert E. Chambliss was identified as planting multiple sticks of dynamite under the steps of the Church. All of the windows were blown out of the church except a single stained glass depicting Christ leading little children. Chambliss was only charged with possession a box of dynamite and convicted and sentenced to only 6 months and fined $100. It wasn't until 1977, twenty-five years later that Chambliss who was retired was convicted and sentenced to life in prison. In 2000, two others who were complicit with Chambliss were convicted and sentenced also. But what took so-long. Martin Luther King said that "justice delayed is justice denied." Therefore, history bare witness that justice for Blacks relative to Whites is scrimpy.

Jena Six. Institutional racism was seen in the Jena Six 2006 case where six Black teenagers in Louisiana, physically assaulted a white teenager. Instead of being charged with an assault and battery, the prosecutor decided to charge the six Blacks each with attempted second degree murder. Only after massive protest by civil rights leaders and residents were the charges changed to assault and batteries or at most aggravated assaults. But this case just shows how grossly racism is ingrained in criminal justice institutions in America.

True assessment of criminals should look at historical crime patterns. The Civil War was caused by Whites who refused to end slavery killing about 600,000 Americans-mostly Whites; WWI started when Archduke Franz Ferdinand of Austria was assassinated, by Gavrilo Princip, A Bosnia-Serb (White), resulting in the death of 16 million people. WWII was started by Hitler, a White Dictator who decided he wanted to kill all Jews and rule the world (Hitler being responsible for the murder of over 6 million Jews). The Gulf War of 2003 resulted from lies about weapons of mass destruction in which after the war, George W. Bush, Dick Cheney and Donald Rumsfeld admitted was based on false intelligence and lies. The Iraq body count was over 100,000. The American body count was close to 4000 (about the same number who perished on 911 at the World Trade Center).

Another test of criminality is to look at the ethnicity of serial killers in America. It is believed that 90-95% of all serial killers are White, including Jeffrey Dahmer, Jack the Ripper, the Zodiac Killer, Robert Hansen, Richard Kulinski, H.H. Holmes, Aileen Wuomos, Gary Ridgeway, Richard Rader, Richard Ramirez, (etc.) Most Mass killings in America are by Whites. Therefore, if one wants to objectively explore difference in crime and crime rates between Blacks and Whites multiple crime indexes must be explored, not just statistics that are Kosher to those who aim to put Blacks back in chains, or pump them into the prison industrial complex. Whites (Romans) even killed Jesus. So when Bill O'Riley wrote his book on "Killing Jesus," he should have placed emphasis on the fact that a Black man helped Jesus to the cross but white Men killed Jesus.

Racial Profiling in the Jury & Criminal Justice Systems. In the Trayvon Martin case, Rachel Jeantel was demonized as not being intelligent, yet it was later reported that she speaks three languages (English, Spanish and Haitian Creole). Did the jury demonize her character? In the Michael Brown case, Officer Wilson did not operate, as a peace officer but as a gangster. He did not seek to de-escalate but to escalate. When he radioed in he said "shots fired" he never said officer in distress and needs assistance. This is because he was the aggressor. Finally, if there was just one juror who said that Michael Brown had his hands- up end of story, it goes to trial. Evidence shows that there were several witness who said Michael Brown had his hands up, yet the prosecutors did not advocate for an indictment and structural racism caused group- think and prevent the jurors from rendering justice and an indictment.

Implicit Association Test. The IAT was developed by Greenwald & colleagues (2009). It involves several computer tasks of associating or matching various word or attributes to other categories like Black &

White. Results indicated that people have more positive associations for Whites people than Blacks people. A similar study was conducted by Gentry and colleagues (2008) at Hanover College. They found that participants in their study repeatedly paired negative objects, weapons, to African American faces while pairing the positive or neutral objects, to Caucasian faces. This suggests subconscious racism and discrimination against Black, even when Whites think they are not racist. This also seems to explain why jurors could fail to indict White police officers who kill unarmed Blacks. It seems to explain how people can see the video of Eric Garner being choked to death and still claim that he was not choked, or if he didn't resist the law he would still be alive.

"The cup of endurance has spilled over" (Martin Luther King, Jr., 1963). Many mislabeled the recent protests in Ferguson, New York, California, Cleveland and all across America, as riots. However, legal justice denied in the courts will be gained through what Martin Luther King Jr. called social justice. The church has been pioneers in organizing people to protest injustices in America. Today churches, civil rights and human rights groups organize in efforts to address police brutality, racial inequity, income disparities and voting rights challenges. The killings by the KKK in 1963 where Blacks were attempting to march from Selma to Montgomery to protest injustices in voting rights caused King to state that the "cup of endurance has spilled over." It was reported that King was visibly angry that marchers including John Lewis, Hosea Williams and scores of other were brutally beaten. Even after marchers retreated back to Brown's Chapel, where the march started, they were still beaten. Viola Liuzzo was shot and killed by the KKK in Montgomery for transporting and assisting Blacks in the Selma to Montgomery march. Rev James Reeb was murdered and Jimmie Lee Jackson was shot by a state trooper, as he marched at night.

Racial Profiling in Educational Institutions is not a new phenomenon. Society is quick to forget how Ruby Bridges at age 6 years old was cursed by adult Whites in Louisiana, as she attempted to integrate the public schools. A White adult female made a black-coffin and told Ruby that she was going to put her in it. Education in America has historically been traumatizing for Blacks. In addition, Zero tolerance programs, instituted to control Blacks makes educational life tormenting. Zero Tolerance programs are disproportionately applied against Blacks and Hispanics. In 2008, the American Psychological Association's Zero Tolerance Task Force found that not only did Zero Tolerance programs not work, but caused more harm than good. They created conflicts between schools and the juvenile justice system and hindered adolescents' development. In essence they demonized Black children as criminals. Finally Zero Tolerance program unjustly pump Black into the Prison Industrial Complex.

It is my opinion that in higher education, Blacks are also profiled, as being less intelligent and lazy, even when they work harder and perform better. Many White institutions can't identify with the Black culture. White Institutions often have political, philosophical and personal conflicts in accepting Black student's research and success. Wilder (2013) made a compelling case that historical White institutions were partners in the slave industry, by accepting endowments in exchange for promoting scientific racism and White Supremacy ideologies. It's this implicit racism that's the foundation of institutional racism. And any student, faculty or administrator who dare advocated for diversity and inclusion will be viewed as criminals and will receive the full-wrath of the Institution heaped upon his or her head.

Many institutions today pride themselves with having humanistic ideas. But let us not forget that the original humanistic institutions and humanistic philosophers have their roots in the period of slavery. Humanist psychology has its roots, during the period of Jim Crow. Postmodern Humanists who have not shifted gears into understanding and integrating diversity and inclusion into their humanist ideas are talking with a fork tongue. According to Helms (2008), Whites must confront their own hidden skeletons of racism to become authentic and mature. In my opinion, before anyone dare enter into the self-actualizing atmosphere, he or she must confront their implicit or explicit issues of racism head on. By confronting, I mean, actively, advocating for equality everywhere.

Chapter I
High Tech Lynching

In this chapter, I address my interest in the research question: What is the experience of Black men relative to criminal stereotypes? I describe how my past experience has led to my current interest in this topic as well as the social and clinical relevance of this research.

This study examines the socially constructed stereotype of the Black man as criminal. As a result of this stereotyping, Black American men have been deprived of basic rights and immunities enjoyed by other citizens (Altman, 2010). Through years of oppressive trauma, such as slavery, Black Codes, Jim Crow laws, and institutional racism, Black men have too often been viewed as criminals without justification (Gabbidon, Greene, & Yong, 2002). It is of great concern that many criminal behaviors are improperly attributed to Black men as a means of societal scapegoating, in efforts to justify oppressive ideologies (Goldman & Gallen, 1992). Denial of these problems only blocks the healing and recovery process of both Black men and society in general. Therefore, this narrative inquiry will explore criminal stereotyping from the African American man's perspective.

My intention in taking on this study is to examine the experience of Black men as it relates to being marginalized through stereotype as being criminals. In limiting my study to Black men, I sought to gain insight into their stories. It seems that often the stories concerning what or who is criminal are told from the perspective of institutions and the legal systems. Therefore, my aim is to gain greater insight into the disproportionate number of Black males in the criminal justice system. I also desire to understand the impact of this criminalization on Black men clinically.

Personal and Professional Relevance

As a former special assistant prosecutor, I learned that a major goal of the criminal justice system is to bring to justice those who have committed a crime against the community by violating individual rights and harming the property and peace of others. But I also learned that justice is not always blind. Moreover, I have seen a close connection between poverty and incarceration. But what concerned me even more is the connection between being Black and being poor. Therefore, if being Black means being poor and being poor means being incarcerated, then crime must be connected. Does being Black cause one to commit crimes, or does being poor cause one to be viewed as a criminal, which results in the commission of crimes, incarceration, or both? The answer to this syllogism will be explored in this study.

I was raised in a Christian family, so I was told that it is important to be kind to our neighbors and to help them if they are in need. As a child my parents told me that Jesus once said how we treat others is how we treat him and the wealthy should share their wealth with the poor. Therefore, I grew up believing that it is our responsibility to love our neighbors as our self and not to marginalize them. My interest as it relates to this study is whether this same benevolence is at play relative to Black men and criminal stereotypes.

My interest in the experience of Black men relative to criminal stereotypes developed as a result of seeing many Black males from poor neighborhoods disproportionately involved in the criminal justice system. I also am concerned with whether this trend is consistent across economic levels for Black men. I myself have been followed by various people in authority without cause.

I have seen many Black men struggle just to gain basic rights and dignity but criminalized for their efforts. Is this as an epidemic? I am concerned that the plight of Black men associated with criminal stereotypes may be rooted in American culture and feel that it will take our entire society working together in a win-win effort to cure this epidemic. However, this problem seems to be seen by some as only an issue for African-Americans.

Professionally, I feel a deep connection and responsibility to join in understanding the phenomenon of stereotyping Black men as criminal. Lastly, I venture to address whether other Black men have had similar experiences and to understand how their experiences can help broaden the scientific literature of criminology relative to Black men. This study will also provide insight into whether viewing Black men as criminals influence them to behave more criminally. Are Black men treated differently than White men, as it relates to being a criminal?

Social and Clinical Relevance

Throughout American history, Blacks have been given labels in efforts to oppress them (Metzl, 2010). For example, in 1851, physician Samuel Cartwright coined the term drapetomania to define Black men who escaped slavery (White, 2002). The term protest psychosis was coined in 1968 by psychiatrists Walter Bromberg and Franck Simon, who argued that Black Power views drove Black men insane (Metzl, 2010).

The idea that Black men are expected to be criminal and dangerous are ethnic stereotypes in the United States and United Kingdom; this is what is called the criminal-Blackman (Gabbidon et al., 2002). Katheryn Russell-Brown (1998) used the stereotypic myth "criminalblackman," to describe how people associate young Black men with crime in the American culture. She further added that the Black male is portrayed as a "symbolic pillager of all that is good."

The current study looks at the uses and misuses of attributing criminal labels to Black men. The goal of the study is not to argue that Black men have no criminal behaviors, but to provide a personal and social context to better understand Black men, relative to perceived criminality, and the impact that these stereotypes have on their experience. It also attempts to clarify what impact these stereotypes have on Black men psychologically and socially. Exploring the experience of Black men may help researchers and clinicians understand how to break this cycle of criminal stereotypes and to identify what is necessary to prevent Black men from being unfairly incarcerated.

Black men are often characterized as being violent and aggressive in the media and society (Rome, 2004). Where are the philosophies, psychologies, social activism, and multicultural efforts that aid Black men in discovering their human potential? It appears all too often that when Black men have economic and emotional problems these difficulties are interpreted as conduct problems (Rome, 2004). Are psychologists too quick to jump the gun and see Black men as criminals?

Even though Abraham Maslow (1944) did not directly address the impact of society on individual actualization, his hierarchy of needs model is helpful in understanding the relationship between access to basic needs and overall psychological and social success in Black men. It appears that societal conditions that would allow the average American to self-actualize are less available to Black men.

Maslow's hierarchy is a way of conceptualizing how humans often prioritize their physical, social, and psychological needs. At the bottom of the hierarchy are the basic needs of a human being: air, food and water. The next level is security and stability. These two steps are important to the physical survival of the person. Once individuals have basic nutrition, shelter, and safety, they attempt to accomplish more. The third level of need is love and belonging, which are psychological needs; when individuals have taken care of themselves physically, they are ready to share themselves with others. The fourth level is achieved when individuals feel comfortable with what they have accomplished. This is the esteem level, the level of success and status. The top of the hierarchy, self-actualization, occurs when individuals reach a state of harmony and understanding (Maslow, 1944).

Not only have criminal stereotypes deprived Black men of equal rights, but they have also affected their self-esteem. It appears that among all groups in America, Black men have extreme difficulty in reaching the highest levels of Maslow's hierarchy (Goldman & Gallen, 1992). It also appears that the deprivation of basic needs of Black males and years of oppressive trauma through slavery, Jim Crow laws, Black Codes, and institutional racism have forced many Black males onto a path of criminal behaviors (Pickren & Dewsbury, 2002).

By better understanding the experience of Black men in regards to the criminal stereotype and the impact it has on their psychological and social functioning, clinicians, academics, and policy makers will be better equipped to empower these men and help them to fully actualize themselves, their families and communities, and society-at-large. It is also a goal to identify potential barriers and strategies around these barriers that can be used to inform psychological treatments of Black men.

The Research Question

What is the experience of African American men relative to being stereotyped as criminal?

Definition of terms

Experience

According to Corsini (1999) "an experience is one lived through, or undergone, as opposed to one imagined or thought about. It is knowledge or skill resulting from instructive events and practice" (p. 351). Rogers (1959) defines experience as including "all that is going on within the envelope of the organism at any given moment, which is potentially available." For this study, experience is described as the personal felt reality of the individual telling the story.

African American and Black identifications

Du Bois (1965) addressed the issues of dual consciousness concerning the dilemma that the Negro had with being an American while maintaining solidarity with his African roots. Anderson (2003) argues that the conscious effort of slave-holders to obliterate the distinct African identity of African people resulted in psychological difficulties and ideological conflicts among African Americans. Furthermore, Compton (1993) held that Blacks have always deliberated over whether to seek the acceptance of identification with Whites or to adopt and declare a Black or African identity distinct from European Americans (p. 22).

The terms Black, African American, and people of color have been used interchangeably (Compton, 1993) due to disagreements among African-American people as to the appropriate usage. The word Black is associated with interest in Black identification that resulted from the

Black power movement during the late 1960s and early 1970s; it focused on racial pride and the creation of Black political and cultural institutions to nurture and promote Black collective interests and advance Black values (Philogène, 1999, p. 8). Various names have been used to identify people in America of African descent in an effort to change the perception of the group and interrelations. There has been much conflict over the development of the names slave, Negro, Colored, Black, Afro-American, Person of Color, and finally, African American.

The term African American is currently used most because it has a broader appeal. It shifts the emphasis from race to culture and fits better into the multicultural philosophy. The primary purpose of an ethnic name is to find an identity that will promote pride and self-esteem (Philogène, 1999). The concept of African American also addresses the dual consciousness within the Black community relative to being of African descent but also being American (Philogène, 1999, p. 17).

On the other hand, the concept of African American is not the best term to address the primary trait upon which African Americans are profiled: being Black. This study operates on a premise that Black men are criminally stereotyped because they are not White, and they are perceived as non-Americans. The term Black was used during the Civil Rights, Black Power, and Affirmative Action eras to equate with the term White. It gave Blacks a sense of pride and culture but reminded Blacks that there was still work to do relative to race issues, equal rights and equal opportunities.

Therefore, for the purpose of this study, the term Black will be used because it places more emphasis on a common characteristic of a subculture that is targeted as being criminal. In essence, when a person is profiled, what matters is the tone of being Black. Therefore the word Black will be emphasized for this study.

Man

From the ancient Judeo-Christian perspective, a man is an adult creation of God in the image of God. Man is seen as having his own consciousness and will but is created as a moral being without criminal intent. Man was created at the top of the food chain (Eichrodt & Smith, 1972). This perspective sees man originally as created without criminal intent but fallen to the state of having a sinful nature.

From a scientific and anthropological perspective, man originated about 1.6 million years ago and is from the homo-sapiens species, which are considered primates from the hominidae family, the homo sapiens-sapiens sub-species, and the only living species of the genus homo (Goodman et al., 1990). From a genetics perspective, a male is identified as having an XY designation for the 23rd chromosome, which is the sex chromosome (Tower & Arbeitman, 2009). If the sperm carries a Y chromosome that fertilizes the egg, the result is masculine. If the sperm which fertilizes the egg carries an X chromosome, the result is feminine.

In order to understand masculinity and femininity from a postmodern perspective, gender must be considered. Gender is a concept that not only considers biology but also reflects a person's lifestyle (Haig, 2004). A biological female could adopt the gender of a male and a biological male could adopt the gender of a female. Sex is the biological determination relative to hormones of either an XX female or an XY male.

For the purpose of this study, man will be defined as an adult who identifies with the masculine identity.

Criminal

A criminal is a person charged with and convicted of a crime by the state. A crime is an act in violation of a public right or duty (Garner, 2009). The word criminal is derived from the word crime, which comes from the Latin root cemo, which means, I decide, I give judgment. The Latin word comes from the Ancient Greek word Krima which refers to an intellectual mistake or an offense against the community, rather than a private or moral wrong (Garner, 2009). During the 13th century, crime was seen as sinful. Implicit in this definition is the legislative process of what a crime is and who should be prosecuted under what conditions.

For the purpose of this study, a criminal is a person justifiably charged with and or convicted of a crime.

Stereotype

This concept refers to a way of thinking, behaving, and/or believing that may or may not be based in reality (Judd & Park, 1993). "Stereotypes are categorical assumptions that all members of a given group have a particular trait. Stereotypes could be positive or negative, simple or differentiated and held with or without confidence and vary in their degree" (Shiraev & Levy, 2007, p. 299).

For the purpose of this study, a stereotype is an assumption that all members of a given group have a particular trait.

Summary

This chapter has presented an historical context for and the social and clinical relevance of the question that has been chosen for this study. The next chapter presents a review of the literature, a discussion of the relevance of the data to this investigation, and the position of my research in the field of psychology.

Chapter II
The pathological Development of Racial Profiling in America

This discussion will begin by exploring a brief history of Blacks in America, sex and gender, the history of mental health diagnoses, Antisocial Personality Disorder, and the negative consequences of stereotyping Black males as antisocial. Additional relevant areas discussed are critical race theory, power, slavery, Jim Crow and Black Codes, affirmative action, aggression and males, the concept of criminalblackman, increased mental health diagnoses among Black men, increased incarceration rates for Black men, socioeconomic problems, and physical health problems associated with criminal stereotypes of Black males.

History of Blacks in America

During the early colonial period, slavery existed in America as a form of involuntary labor for African Americans. While there were some Africans in America before the beginning of slavery, most Africans were forcefully migrated to America from West and Central Africa between 1619 and 1865 (Palmer, 2002). Because fewer Europeans were coming to the colonies between the 16th to the 19th centuries, an estimated 12 million Africans were shipped as slaves to the Americas. Between 597,000 and 645,000 slaves made it to the U.S. According to the 1860 Census, the number of slaves in the U.S. grew to four million. After the American Revolution, the Northern states abolished slavery and Congress prohibited slavery in the Northwest Territories (Behrendt, Richardson, & Eltis, 1999). Yet with the emergence of the cotton industry in the 1800s, slavery was allowed to extend to the Southwestern Territories, even though the import and export of slaves were made illegal in 1807. The South continued to argue for slavery, while the abolition movement in the North advocated against it (Behrendt et al., 1999).

Slavery was a brutal period for Blacks. In her autobiography, Incidents in the Life of a Slave Girl, Jacobs (2003) explained that slaves and their children had no rights. Blacks were sold as animals and were considered chattel, not citizens. Slaves were denied the opportunity to learn to read and write, and medical assistance was extremely limited. Brutality, including rape, could be forced upon slaves with little or no legal recourse. The slaves belonged to their masters and were considered the property of the slave owner, and the children of slaves were also slaves of their masters. Slavery was deeply rooted in society and supported many of the elite education institutions in America (Wilder, 2013). Therefore slavery had become, if not explicit, then implicit in the fabric and metaphoric DNA of America. In 1844, Secretary of State John C. Calhoun argued for the extension of slavery, believing that Blacks were incapable of self-care and needed protection for their own mental health (Lence, 1992). Blacks were demonized. Early minstrel shows during the mid-19th century depicted Blacks as ignorant and stupid. Blacks were also portrayed as being lazy, superstitious, happy- go-lucky, and musical (Mahar, 1998).

The Black fight for freedom and civil rights started to influence American moral consciousness during the abolitionist movements that began in the 830s (Ruggles, 2011). Moreover, slavery in America was paradoxical because it exposed America's hypocritical stance towards its most cherished value: freedom. While many Whites in the North had moral objections to slavery, others were afraid that the South was becoming too powerful and independent as a result of its slave labor; therefore, the North started putting pressure on the South to abolish slavery. Compromises between the North and South concerning slavery failed and in 1861 seven, then 11 Southern states seceded from the United States, forming the Confederate States of America (Masur, 2011).

During that time, President Lincoln offered a compromise involving slaves that he hoped would save the Union. He stated, "My paramount object in this struggle is to save the Union, and is not either to save or to destroy slavery. If I could save the Union without freeing any slave I would do it, and if I could save it by freeing all the slaves I would do it; and if I could save it by freeing some and leaving others alone I would also do that. What I do about slavery, and the colored race, I do because I believe it helps to save the Union" (Basler, 1946, p. 652) Moreover, in the Lincoln-Douglas debates, Lincoln indicated that he was against miscegenation and Blacks serving as jurors; he thought Whites were superior to Blacks (Gates, 2009). The Confederates rejected his offer, which resulted in the Civil War. This demonstrates that, even as President Lincoln fought to free the slaves, he too had racist tendencies common to that historical time period and perceptions about Blacks relative to Whites.

Blacks fought with the Union, resulting in the South being defeated after a half million lives were lost from the combined Union and Confederate armies. That number was about equivalent to the number of slaves that originally landed in the United States. In 1863, the Emancipation Proclamation was signed. In 1865, the war ended and the 13th Amendment was passed, abolishing slavery and freeing the slaves. The Civil War legally ended slavery but not the racism supporting it.

White Supremacy

Race was a term constructed by Europeans to defend their oppression and domination of others. In the eighteenth century, Germans promoted the idea that Caucasians were more beautiful than other races using pseudoscientific arguments. They saw northern Europeans, "Saxons," "Anglo-Saxons," and "Teutons" as superior, more beautiful, and better rulers (Painter, 2010).

This notion of White Supremacy was furthered by Madame de Stael and Thomas Carlyle (Painter, 2010). When this race theory reached North America, White supremacy was lobbied for by Ralph Waldo Emerson (Painter, 2010). He claimed that Anglo-Saxons were the real Americans and excluded all ethnic groups not of Protestant, Northern European background. This notion of scientific White supremacy became popular throughout the United States. The acceptance of other groups (e.g., Irish, Italians, Polish, etc.) as being real, "White" Americans, wasn't truly seen until far into the 20th century. Politics, economics, skull sizes, the powerful eugenics movement, and highly biased intelligence tests were used to keep those considered lesser people excluded from the privileges and amenities of "true" Americans (Painter, 2010).

Helms (2007 explained the psychology of White identity formation. She indicated that White people are born into a society in which they are told that it is better to be White. She explained that the foundation of White identity is what is called contact schema by which people pretend to be innocent, ignorant, or neutral regarding race or racial issues (p. 31). Helms added that contact identity breaks down when Whites are faced with racial issues. The primary constructs of contact schema are denial of racism and the claim of color blindness (p. 31). The second schema of White identity is disintegration. This schema is used when denial breaks down and confusion sets in. At this point one becomes aware that he/she is White and that one has privileges not afforded to Blacks. Whites also realize that in order to maintain that status and be accepted by other Whites, Blacks and non-White groups must be treated as inferior. In order to deal with this dissonance, reality is distorted and victims of racism are blamed. The next schema of White identity formation is to become skilled at the complex distortion of reality with regard to racism; this is called reintegration. The final stages are pseudo-independent (helping Blacks to become more like Whites), immersion/emersion (trying to see ones role in promoting racism) is developing a nonracist White identity, which is a difficult hurdle and requires admitting to one's racism and autonomy taking the time, commitment, and effort to remove and prevent racist tendencies (Helms, 2007). Failure to achieve a health White identity will result in developing Racial Profiling Disorder.

Jim Crow and Black Codes

State and local Black Codes immediately followed the 13th Amendment in 1865. They reiterated the claims of the Blacks' inferior status and the superior status of Whites. Finally, Black Codes did not just extend to the Southern states; Northern states also discriminated against Blacks. These laws prohibited Blacks from marrying Whites. Black Codes in the South and North were even harsher to Blacks than many slaveholders were to their slaves (Cohen, 1976).

The Jim Crow laws from 1876 to 1965 required de jure separation of races in all public facilities in the previous Confederate Southern states. These laws required literal and explicit separation of Blacks and Whites and were enforced. This segregation was seen in housing, banking, employment, schools, transportation, restaurants, and all other areas of civil life (Cohen, 1976).

Civil Rights Movement

The Civil Rights Act of 1866 is not considered a part of the civil rights movement because it had no significant effect for Blacks on their life, liberty, and pursuit of happiness. It simply did not have the enforcement of law (Curry, 1996). The civil rights movement covers the period when the demand for civil rights was being enforced. It is usually thought to have occurred between 1950 and 1980, although the initial movement was between 1955 and 1968 (Curry, 1996). While many people were instrumental in the movement, one of its most important leaders was Dr. Martin Luther King, Jr. The goal of this movement was to make racial discrimination illegal and to grant Blacks legitimate voting rights. Some of the main events were the Montgomery Bus Boycott (1955–1956), the Greensboro sit-ins in North Carolina (1960), the "I have a Dream" speech in 1963, and the Selma to Montgomery March in 1965

(Goldman & Gallen, 1992). This movement involved civil disobedience and nonviolent means of opposing racial discrimination. Some of the strategies used were demonstrations, vigils, petitions, strikes, go-slows, boycotts, emigration movements, sit-ins, occupations, and the creation of parallel institutions of government.

The civil rights movement resulted in the passage of the Civil Rights Act of 1964, which banned discrimination based on "race, color, religion, or national origin" in employment practices and public accommodations. The Voting Rights Act of 1965 restored and protected voting rights. The Immigration and Nationality Services Act of 1965 dramatically opened entry of the U.S. to immigrants other than traditional European groups (Goluboff, 2007). The Fair Housing Act of 1968 banned discrimination in the sale or rental of housing. Consequently, African Americans were elected to multiple offices in the South and throughout the U.S. and there was renewed excitement in America for Blacks (Goluboff, 2007).

Some of the effects of slavery, racism, Jim Crow, and Black Codes were indirectly measured during the civil rights era through research by a famous Black psychologist, Kenneth B. Clark, and his wife, Mamie Clark. They are best known for research on Black children's self-concepts, which led to their involvement in ending racial segregation in schools (Pickren & Dewsbury, 2002). Drs. Mamie and Kenneth Clark also testified in the Briggs v. Elliot cases. Those cases rolled into the case of Brown v. Board of Education (1954). In that landmark case, Clark addressed racial discrimination and its impact on Black identity (Asante, 2002).

The Clarks' testimony in this case stemmed from their experiments that grew out of Mamie master's thesis, which investigated the perception of skin color on attributes of self-worth, such as intelligence and beauty. The Clarks published three major papers between 1939 and 1940 on children's self-perception related to race. Their studies found contrasts among children attending segregated schools in Washington, DC, versus those in integrated schools in New York. The Clarks found that Black children often preferred to play with White dolls over Black dolls. When asked to fill in a human figure with the color of their own skin, Black children frequently chose a lighter shade than what was accurate. The children also attributed beauty to the White dolls but perceived the Black dolls as bad and ugly (Butler, 2009).

The Clarks' work is important because it provided psychological evidence for Black experience in America, demonstrating how that experience affected self-esteem in children. Kenneth Clark concluded that discrimination has a significant impact on Black children (Butler, 2009). The Clarks' work contributed to the ruling of the U.S. Supreme Court in which it was determined that de jure racial segregation in public education was unconstitutional. In that 1954 decision, Chief Justice Earl Warren stated: to separate those "Black" from others of similar age and qualifications solely because of their race generates feelings of inferiority as to their status in the community that may affect their hearts and minds in a way unlikely to ever be undone. (Christman, 1959, p. 121)

In Brown v. Board of Education of Topeka (1954) the U.S. Supreme Court reversed the Plessey v. Ferguson ruling of 1896, holding that separate is inherently unequal. The Clarks' social action research on integration was significant to this ruling. In 1969, Dr. Clark was the first African American and non-White president of the American Psychological Association (APA). Clark was also concerned with how standards of the past have been used to oppress and depress Black Americans. He was involved in social action rallies and protests against segregation. His work is still significant in understanding the critical factors that have shaped the identity and experience of the Black Americans. At his eulogy in 2005, the President of the American Psychological Association, Ronald F. Levant, indicated that Kenneth Clark was "arguably the most influential psychologist of the 20th century, especially in applying psychological principles to break down barriers to public school desegregation"

(Harper, 2005, p. 37).

The civil rights movement made significant contributions to race relations; it unmasked White supremacist philosophies that have shaped American culture (Levy, 1998). The civil rights movement also caused an examination in the U.S. culture of the morality of treatment of Blacks. Consequently, several civil right laws were passed to enforce the 13th, 14th, and 15th Amendments. The civil rights movement empowered Blacks to not only believe in their dreams but also motivated them to confront oppression in an effort to obtain their dreams and aspirations. As a result, Blacks and Whites are more integrated in employment, housing, and education. There are, however, areas still at issue (Levy, 1998).

Affirmative action initiatives enacted to enforce civil rights are now being taken away (Meyer, 2004). Civil rights organizations are at work to counter setbacks, including a provision of the 15th Amendment that prevents traditional Jim Crow states from significantly altering election laws without consent of the U.S. government. This setback occurred when section 4 of this amendment was overturned by the U.S. Supreme Court in Shelby County v. Holder (2013). Moreover, civil rights advocates are addressing issues related to race being used as a factor in college admission. This issue is currently being challenged in the Federal Courts after the U.S. Supreme Court, in a seven-to-one vote, remanded the Fisher v. University of Texas at Austin (2013) case to a lower court with instructions to address the issues of affirmative action. Civil rights advocates are faced with issues of racial profiling laws by police agencies, seen in the New York Stop, Frisk, and Question policy (Bruinis, 2013). Moreover, civil rights advocates are challenged by efforts that profile and criminalize Hispanic immigrants (Blair, 2011).

Critical Race Theory

Critical Race Theory (CRT) was first formulated in the 1970s by a group of lawyer-activists and scholars across disciplines. The first conference was held in 1989. The CRT founders were concerned that the civil rights movement was moving in reverse. Early pioneers were Derrick Bell, Alan Freeman, and Richard Delgado. Patriarchs in the Critical Race Theory movement were Antonio Gramsci, Jacques Derrida, Sojourner Truth, Frederick Douglass, W.E.B. Du Bois, Cesar Chavez, Martin Luther King, Jr., and the Black Power and Chicano movements of the 60s and early 70s. CRT was also influenced by the feminist movement (Delgado & Stefanic, 2000). CRT theory looks at the effects of society and culture on race, law, and power relations (Yosso, 2006). It sees racism as ingrained in American culture. CRT is concerned that Whites view themselves as superior to Blacks and seek to control and grant Blacks only limited power. CRT also sees racism as the belief that Whites are privileged and believe that they must preserve their power in society (Delgado & Stefanic, 2000).

Power is defined as the ability of an individual to exercise and/or control authority (Shiraev & Levy, 2007, p. 119). Laws, institutions, and culture affect how power is distributed. And the way power is distributed affects the way a person is likely to behave in a given culture. CRT examines the misuse of power at the expense of minority groups. In efforts to maintain power, minorities are deprived of basic rights, privileges, and amenities at the hands of the majority population. CRT also examines the use of stigma to justify limitation of resources, wealth, and power distribution to minority populations (Yosso, 2006). Finally, CRT not only attempts to understand how a society functions along racial lines and hierarchies but also aims to change society for the better (Delgado & Stefanic, 2000).

There are multiple splinter groups that were connected in the initial CRT focus. These include, but are not limited to, Latino, American Indian, and Asian populations and organizations. These groups were concerned about immigration and discrimination based on national origin and how critical race theory impacts it. American Indian scholars addressed indigenous rights, land claims, and sovereignty (Delgado & Stefanic, 2000).

Critical race theory also recognizes the concept of differential racialization, which explains how the dominant society racializes various minority groups at different times to serve its own benefit. It may discriminate against one minority group but favor another for employment purposes. Which groups are racialized can change over time. For example, in one period of American history, Blacks were often viewed as simple minded and happy-go-lucky. Today Blacks are often viewed as aggressive and violent (Delgado & Stefanic, 2000).

Another concept from CRT is intersectionality or anti-essentialism. This suggests that each group has its own unique origins of oppression and that no group has a single identity; each group is made up of multiple identities based, in part, on social group affiliations like ethnicity, class, religion, sexual identity and gender, and similar experiences (Gutiérrez-Jones, 2001). For instance a Black man may experience criminal profiling and poverty, whereas a Black woman may feel sexualized but not criminalized. This often results in conflicts and split loyalties. Yet what all oppressed groups have in common is what is called the "voice of color," which suggests that because Blacks, Latinos, Asians, and American Indians have their own unique histories of oppression, they are competent to speak about race and racism. CRT is a legal storytelling movement that encourages all persons of color, including Blacks, to retell their lived experiences with racism and the legal system (Delgado & Stefanic, 2000).

Dr. Demetrius E. Ford Ph. D. J.D., Psy.D.

Stereotyping

The word "stereotype" comes from combining two Greek words: stereos, meaning "solid," and typos, meaning "the mark of a blow," or more generally "a model." Stereotypes were therefore referred to as solid models. The initial meaning of the term in English referred to a metal plate used to print pages, thus suggesting a connotation of rigidity and duplication, a stamping of objects into sameness (Schneider, 2005).

The term stereotype was first coined in modern psychology by Walter Lippman in 1922. A stereotype is a thought about a person that may not be based in reality. He described stereotypes as imagining things before they are experienced. Lippman (1922) indicated that a person is gullible when using stereotypes and that these preconceptions and mental structures were often used by individuals to maintain a certain status in society. Moreover, he indicated that stereotypes were like seeing with a diseased eye or through color-coated lenses.

Lippman (1922) explained how Aristotle defended slavery in the fourth century B.C. by describing how well the slaves were cared for in comparison to free people. In defending slavery in the Athenian slave culture, Aristotle argued that some people are slaves by nature while others are free. Aristotle added that slaves are destined to become the chattel of another person; therefore, whoever happens to be a slave is by nature a slave. He also stated that some people are made for servitude and some are made for civil labor (Lippman, 1922). Lippman concluded that Aristotle's statements are worthless and not logical but are rather a stereotype used to maintain the oppression evident in ancient Athenian culture.

Katz and Braly (1933) explored issues associated with content, consensus, and attributes among ethnic and national stereotypes. They viewed stereotypes as cultural representations of a group. In their research, they divided 125 Princeton students into two groups that were then asked to rate various ethnic groups on desirability of traits. It was discovered that negative traits were ascribed to Negros, while positive traits were given to other ethnicities. Some of the traits chosen most for Negroes were lazy, happy-go-lucky, ignorant, and musical. Whites were described as industrious, progressive, and ambitious, and the Chinese were described as intelligent. In conclusion, the researchers explained that these stereotypes are rooted in ignorance and groupthink. Follow up studies (e.g., Gilbert, 1951; Karlins, Kauffman, & Walters, 1969) found that Blacks were viewed less negatively, but still not as positively as Whites.

Stereotypes are used to justify certain behaviors directed at minority groups in efforts to maintain power in society (Fiske, 1993). These stereotypes are the basis of minorities being perceived as inferior and incompetent (Bell & Nkomo, 2001). When Whites internalize their stereotypes, Whites' marginalizing becomes more aggressive and pervasive, such as viewing Blacks as less intelligent than Whites (Leslie, 1991).

In the 1940s, research focused on stereotypes against the Jews; this anti-Semitism was evidence of a more deeply-rooted ethnocentrism (Schneider, 2005). Towards the end of the 1940s, the concept of the Authoritarian Personality was developed by Adorno, who suggested that the authoritarian personality seeks total allegiance from another to their authority and uses oppressive means if necessary to gain submission (Adorno. Frenkel-Brunswik, & Levinson, 1950). Adorno and colleagues developed the F Scale for fascism; they concluded that individuals who scored high on the F scale had a very strict upbringing, put others into categories, saw themselves as superior to others, and thus have the Authoritarian Personality. Authoritarians enjoy authority and are typically conservative and intolerant of behaviors that go against their principles Adorno, (1950).

Allport (1979) saw stereotypes as projections of negative features of the self and unresolved conflicts. From this insight, Allport developed the concept of the prejudiced personality, which he understood to be congruent with the authoritarian personality. He contended that the prejudiced personality evinces a weak ego, is insecure, and perceives threat. Allport further indicated that stereotypes are an aspect of cognitive structures that attempt to categorize things according to held values. He added that the unprejudiced person is more likely to use "differentiated categories," those that allow for exceptions and individual variation. On the other hand, those with a prejudiced personality are less likely to be able to achieve this task (Allport, 1979).

Research on stereotypes during 1970s and 1980s focused on the attribution theory, which holds that negative characteristics of out-group members are attributed to personal factors, while negative dispositions of in-group members are attributed to situational factor (Pettigrew, 1979). According to Pettigrew (1979), Hindus and Muslims attributed external causes for their group members' negative acts but internal causes for those that were positive.

Schneider (2005) performed a comprehensive investigation of stereotypes and discovered negative, social-cultural stereotypes but also positive aspects of stereotypes as abstract schemas. Abstract thinking was referred to as cognitive schemas. These stereotype schemas are generalizations used to process information quickly about others and the environment. Consequently, it was argued that more insight is gained when stereotypes are analyzed, as opposed to shunned (Schneider, 2005).

Cinnerela (1998) looked at the relationship between stereotypes and context. This researcher hypothesized that the ratings of in-groups would be positive while those of the out-groups would be negative. In essence, the British would rate their countrymen more favorably than

Italians, and Italians would rate Italians more favorably than the British. British and Italian national identities were measured for favorability by 114 students from the University of London. They were given questions to rate their feelings about the British, Italians, and Europeans. It was discovered that manipulation of the stereotype rating context had a significant impact on outcome. The in-group British rated themselves more favorably than the out-group Italians. Conversely, the in-group Italians rated themselves more favorably than the out-group British. Thus, each group rated themselves more favorably as hypothesized. When assessing favorability between their countries or continents, the British and Italians rated themselves more favorably when comparing themselves to Europeans (Cinnerella, 1998).

Racial Stereotypes

Throughout the 20th century, there have been documented cases of racial stereotypes in America. The historical responsiveness of stereotypes to changing contexts in justifying behavior is perhaps most strongly documented in Americans' attitudes toward the Japanese. Successive samples of Princeton students depicted the Japanese as intelligent, industrious, and progressive in 1933; but they were depicted as imitative, sly, and nationalistic in the wake of the Second World War (Gilbert, 1951). Later, in the 1960s, the Japanese were viewed as industrious, ambitious, and efficient (Karlins, Coffman & Walters, 1969).

Allport (1979) discovered that race is a social attitude propagated among the public by exploiting class to stigmatize some groups as inferior. This is done to justify exploiting the group and the group's resources (Allport, 1979, p. 209). In efforts to determine if there was a difference between positive and negative traits associated with Blacks and Whites, Gaertner and McLaughlin (1983) conducted a study in which participants, White college students, were asked to associate positive and negative words with White and Black people to determine if there were differences in the time it would take to do the task relative to the two populations.

They discovered that there was no significant difference in the time it took to ascribe negative traits to Blacks and Whites. However, everyone ascribed more positive traits to Whites. In addition, it was discovered that, while these college students took no longer to give negative traits to Blacks, they did ascribe positive characteristics to Whites. These researchers, however, failed to address why more positive traits were ascribed to Whites than Blacks. The Clarks' experiments explained that historical racial discrimination negatively impacted Black self-esteem, caused Blacks to see Whites as more positive than themselves, and caused Whites to see Blacks more negatively (Asante, 2002).

Martinez, Piff, and Mendonza-Denton (1993) indicated that anti-Hispanic stereotypes have origins in the American West when Hispanics were colonized, were forced to perform semi-slave labor, and were raped, tortured, and lynched because they were believed to be inept and lazy. This historical point is important because it seems to provide a more in-depth context to the character of a culture that has a pattern of stereotyping on the basis of race. A question arising from this historical point is whether the majority population feels obligated to make conclusions about other races out of a need to maintain a certain order by exerting power and limiting the influences of other races.

Stereotypes discourage thinking about the person as an individual and have negative consequences for both Whites and Blacks. Schneider (2005) contended that stereotypes give rise to a lose-lose consequence when, for example, a Black person's hard work is overlooked because of preconceived stereotypes, such as Blacks are lazy. When this happens, often the employer is deprived of a good worker and the Black person is deprived of employment (Schneider, 2005).

Izumi and Hammonds (2007) examined whether negative stereotypes of ethnic groups caused others to also view these groups negatively. In this study, 45 male and 108 female undergraduate students were provided with negative stereotypes about Koreans, Mexicans, and Jews, and then were asked to rate them. It was discovered that the more negative stereotypes given about the groups, the more likely participants would rate the various groups negatively. It was also discovered that the fewer negative descriptions given about various groups, the fewer negative stereotypes would be given by the raters.

In efforts to better understand racial stereotyping, several fMRI studies have been conducted. Activation in the anterior cingulate cortex (the area of the human brain responsible for empathic response to the infliction of the physical and social pain of others) is reduced when viewing people of a different race (Platek, Krill, & Wilson, 2009). Freeman, Schiller, Rule and Ambady (2010) discovered that activity in the medial prefrontal cortex (the area of the human brain implicated in planning complex cognitive behavior, personality expression, decision making, and moderating social behavior) was reduced when viewing social out-groups as opposed to in-groups. Schreiber and Iacobini (2012) designed a study to see what actually happens in the brain when people violate norms. The brains of 19 Republican, 19 Democratic, and 19 Independently-affiliated college students were scanned before and after viewing pictures of African Americans and European Americans violating norms (i.e., acting criminally or being homeless or gang members). Results indicated that the amygdala (activated when one feels threatened, etc.) was activated when both American Europeans and African Americans were viewed violating norms but also when African American were viewed not violating norms. Schreiber and Iacobini (2012) concluded that negative stereotypes of Black men were responsible for the results.

Unnger and Cullen (2012) explored the relationship between racial stereotypes and support for the death penalty. Results indicated that respondents who believed that African Americans and Hispanics were more violent than Whites were more in favor of the death penalty. In efforts to determine if stereotypes are consistent over time, Talbot and Durheim, (2012) studied whether in South Africa there have actually been social and political attitude changes towards Blacks since the end of apartheid. The study acknowledged that 50 years ago apartheid was South Africa's law and required mandatory racial segregation and White minority rule. The authors hypothesized that stereotypes would be responsive to historical changes in the nature of the relations between the groups. In this study, 723 second-year psychology students were asked to indicate their cultural stereotypes or their personal beliefs pertaining to one of the two different groups. The results showed that a new language of group difference had emerged, but that despite this many of the earlier representations and trends of perception persisted. In essence, most of the stereotypes remained. Talbot and Durheim, (2012) indicated that stereotypes may be more trait-like and biological than state-like and environmentally influenced. Their results showed consistency with in-group stereotypes over time.

A study by Berdhal and Min (2012) explored the issues surrounding whether or not East Asians were treated differently when they acted in ways contrary to American societal expectations. A total of 157 East Asians and Whites were interviewed. Participants were asked to give descriptors that depict Asians. Results indicated that East Asians were in fact perceived as more competent than Whites but less warm. It was also discovered that East Asians were stereotyped as being less dominant. Moreover, participants found it less desirable for East Asians to be dominant than Whites. Berdhal and Min's (2012) results suggest that East Asians were as competent and warm as Whites but less dominant than Whites. These results are consistent with how Whites viewed East Asians historically when East Asians received low pay and low status jobs (e.g., cooks, waiters, cashiers, textile workers). Moreover, Berdahl and Min (2012) confirm that Americans still hold stereotypes of East Asians and are not yet ready to be tolerant of them acting differently from traditional American "majority" standards.

Black Stereotypes

In the first of a series of studies, research (e.g., Correll, Park, Judd & Wittenbrink, 2007) investigated the question of whether police officers were more likely to shoot Black criminals than White criminals. The sample consisted of 70 non-Black college freshmen from the University of Chicago. Interviewers were asked to read newspaper articles about Black and White criminals involved in armed and unarmed robberies. Participants were then presented with video games and told to shoot the armed assailant. Half of the targets were Black and half were White. Blacks were shot significantly more times than Whites. In following scenarios the number of White and Black targets with and without guns were changed. Blacks were again shot much more frequently than Whites. It was concluded that exposure to stereotypes regarding Black men as criminals increased the likelihood that they would be shot more than their White counterparts.

The above study is significant in understanding whether racial stereotypes exist relative to Black men being criminal. Moreover, it adds to understanding the phenomenon of the criminal profiling of Black men. This study is also significant because it raises awareness of how the media influences society to stereotype Black men as criminals. It concluded that "stereotypes that link Blacks to being dangerous and criminal can dramatically affect the magnitude of racial bias in the decision to shoot" (Correll et al., 2007, p. 1107). On the other hand, after reading the newspaper article about White criminals there was no increase in decisions to shoot Whites.

Jones and Kaplan (2003) explored the effects of racial stereotypes of Blacks regarding criminal behavior on juror decision-making and information processing strategies. They hypothesized that Whites would be judged more harshly for stereotypical white collar crimes and Blacks would be judged more harshly for stereotypical violent crimes. The participants were 180 European American males and 180 European American females, all college students over 18 years of age. The study was a two factor design that examined Black and White perpetrators of grand-theft auto and embezzlement. Vehicular manslaughter was included as a non-stereotypical crime to establish a baseline. Participants were given basic instructions about the applicable laws. Finally, participants were told to select additional evidence from confirmatory evidence or diagnostic evidence.

Participants were then asked to rate guilt on a Likert scale from 1 to 10 (1 was less likely to be guilty and 10 most likely guilty). Then participants were asked to rate a minimum versus maximum punishment on a Likert scale of 1 to 9 (1 represented minimum and 9 represented maximum). Participants' rating of the attribution of the defendant's behavior due to internal/personality or external/environmental factors was assessed on a Likert scale 1 to 9 (1 represented internal and 9 represented external). Participants also rated the stability of behavior/recidivism on a scale of 1 to 9 (1 represented not at all stable and 9 represented very much stable). Scores were then averaged for three domains: instability, stability, and responsibility. After participants completed this, they were given 10 additional pieces of evidence related to the crimes investigated and were asked to reach a second verdict with more confidence.

Results indicated that Blacks were found guilty more often for more stereotypically violent crimes (Jones & Kaplan, 2003). In the grand-theft auto verdicts, Blacks were found guilty more often than innocent and Whites were judged to be innocent more often than guilty. Whites charged with embezzlement were more often found guilty than innocent. On the other hand, there were no significant differences between guilty and innocent verdicts for Blacks charged with embezzlement. Lastly, race had no effect for the non-stereotypic crimes of vehicular homicide (Jones & Kaplan, 2003). This study raises concern relative to stereotype influence in the criminal justice experience of Black men.

Summary

Blacks are stereotyped in the American criminal justice system. A study exploring if Police officers were more likely to shoot if the perpetrator were Black found that Blacks were more likely to be shot than Whites. Even in cases where Blacks were not carrying guns, they were still shot more often than Whites. (Correll, Park, Judd, & Wittenbrink, 2007). The media stereotyping Black men as violent contribute to the decisions of Whites to shoot Blacks more frequently. This information is essential to understanding the impact of stereotyping Black men and Black men being victims of crime.

Once Blacks are brought into the justice system are they treated with dignity and fairness? Do Blacks receive due process and equal protection? Is there fairness within the courtroom for Blacks? Or are Blacks judged more harshly and traumatized by the courtroom experience? Jones and Kaplan (2003) found that when jurors are given instructions on Blacks and Whites who have committed violent crimes, jurors are more likely to convict Blacks. Moreover, Jurors were more likely to attribute violent acts of Blacks to internal reasons but attributed violent acts of Whites to external causes (Jones & Kaplan, 2003).

Criminalblackman

Criminalblackman is a myth that perpetuates the stereotype that young Black men are criminals (Russell-Brown, 1998). Often when anyone is accosted in a parking lot at a mall from behind and cannot identify the perpetrator, the default perpetrator is a Black man. Because Black men are disproportionately represented as criminals in the media, the image in the minds of White America is that criminal perpetrators are Black men; this is the contention of the criminalblackman theory (Peterson, Lauren, & Krivo, 2006).

Russell-Brown (1998) explained that a racial hoax is perpetrated when a White person fabricates a crime and blames it on a person of another race; this was seen in the Susan Smith, Jesse Anderson, and Charles Stuart cases (Russell-Brown, 1998, p. 70). In all three, Black men were scapegoated for the crimes. Furthermore, while there are hundreds of criminal offenses, attention is mostly given to the eight index offenses (i.e., murder, rape, robbery, aggravated assault, burglary, motor vehicle theft, larceny-theft, and arson) that Black men are mostly charged with and convicted of (Peterson et al., 2006).

In reality Blacks are perceived as being more dangerous criminals but results are surprising. In 2012, Whites accounted for 73.4% of all arrests, 85.8% of all liquor law violations, 85.5% of all drunkenness, 79.2% of all arsons, 77.4% of all sex offenses (excluding forcible rape and prostitutions), 73.6% of all drug abuse violations, 72.6% of all forcible rapes, 70% of all property offenses, 69.3% of stolen property offenses, 68.9% of all disorderly conduct offenses, and 54% of all murders and non-negligent homicides (Uniform Crime Report, 2012). Yet the criminal face portrayed by the media is that of a Black man. The criminalblackman theory is a colonial model that has characterized the Black man as the bogey man. This misperception has diminished the development of rational theoretical explanations within crime and criminology studies (Peterson et al., 2006).

The media contributes significantly to stereotyping the Black man as criminal. For example, Denzel Washington won an Oscar for being the drug dealing police officer in Training Day instead of for one of his many other critically acclaimed roles that weren't criminal in nature. A disproportionate amount of time is spent portraying Black men committing violent crimes compared to White men (Grossman, 2001). This obsession with viewing Black men as criminal started in what is called the blaxploitation films of the 1970s. Blaxploitation films depicted Black males as aggressive, lawless, and violent as a result of their slave experience (Rome, 2004).

Criminalblackman in the Justice System

The drug abuser is one of the common stereotypes related to Black men. However, according to the United States Department of Health and Human Services, only 8% of Blacks have used cocaine compared to 11% of Whites (Rome, 2004). As a result of the alarming, disproportionate portrayal of Black men as deviant, dangerous, and dysfunctional, social scientist T. J. Gibbs has argued that the social media is racist (Rome, 2004).

Another example of the negative effects of Black stereotypes can be seen in the criminal justice system in the disparities of its crack-cocaine sentencing guidelines. Crack cocaine, not the powder cocaine used in the 1980s, was stated to be a drug of choice for Blacks because it was more affordable for poor individuals. Crack was cheaper and therefore more Blacks could purchase it. Consequently, a myth was developed by the media that crack cocaine caused more violent crimes. This propaganda was used to scapegoat Blacks and to declare that they were the primary perpetrators of inner-city crime. Thus, the war on crime was really a war on Blacks. Legislators instituted the 1986 Anti- Drug Abuse Act, which punished users of crack cocaine, mostly Blacks, 100 times more than powder cocaine users, even though the two drugs are chemically identical. Research by Reinarman, Waldorf, Murphy, and Levine (1997) showed that crack users were no more violent than powder cocaine users. Later, legislators argued that this was done for the purpose of enhanced sentencing without justification, amounting to political racism.

This stereotype associated with crack cocaine has been partially corrected with the Obama administration. A congressional commission concluded that crack cocaine users were no more violent than powder cocaine users (Dvorak, 1999; Wytsma, 1994). Subsequently, the Federal sentencing guidelines for crack offenses were changed through the Fair Sentencing Act (Fair Sentencing Act, 2010). The Fair Sentencing Act (FSA) eliminated the huge unjust differences in sentencing between crack and cocaine. Over 80% of the crack cocaine convictions were Black, and their sentences were six times longer than Whites. Using cocaine. The FSA increased the quantities of crack cocaine that trigger the five-year statutory mandatory minimum penalties from five grams to 28 grams. It increased the 10-year mandatory minimums from 50 to 280 grams.

In 2011, the sentencing guidelines were applied retroactively. As a result, approximately 7,152 defendants' crack cocaine sentences were reduced to an average of 37 months. That added up to a decrease of nearly 22,052 cumulative years of federal imprisonment and saved about a billion dollars. Finally, the fact that 85% of those benefitting from this reduction were Black suggests that Blacks have been stereotyped and racialized with regard to crack cocaine prosecutions (U.S. Sentencing Commission, 2014).

The media and society stereotyped Blacks in the 1980s and 1990s as being more violent because many Black cocaine users preferred the crack form of cocaine (because it was cheaper) than other forms. This crack cocaine issue is an example of the stereotyping that Black men experience. Furthermore, this crack cocaine phenomenon used to criminalize and profile Black men suggests a pervasive, stereotypical pattern that is not just seen at the local community level, but also in all branches of the government. Investigation of this phenomenon is essential for adding to and broadening the research literature in criminology and other intersecting disciplines. While the Fair Sentencing

Act reduced the disparity of crack to cocaine use from a ratio of 100 to 1 to a ratio of 18 to 1, the sentencing reduction did not go far enough. The 6th Circuit Court of Appeals indicated that Congress's failure to absolutely correct this racial disparity was tantamount to "intentional subjugation akin to the resurrection of slavery and Jim Crow Laws" (U.S. v. Blewett, 2013).

Another example where we see Black stereotypes at work is in policing. For many years the New York City Police Department operated a stop, question, and frisk policy that stereotyped Black and Hispanic/Latino males. This policy disproportionately implicated Blacks and Hispanics in crime. In essence, this policy allowed the New York City police to conduct stops of the city's residents and visitors and to restrain their freedom, even if only briefly. Over 2.8 million stops were made from 2004 to 2009. Over 50% of the stops were Blacks, 30% were Latino, and only 10% involved Whites, despite the fact that the majority of New York residents are White. The U.S. Federal District for the Southern District of New York struck down the policy, calling it city-sanctioned racial profiling (Harvard Law Review, 2013). An independent monitor was appointed to oversee the city's compliance (Bruinis, 2013). As a result, the New York Police Department is under federal monitoring and some officers must wear body cameras. In addition, the New York City Council installed oversight of the police department, and allows victims to sue the city in state court (Bruinis, 2013).

Stereotyping Black men as criminal results in society's practice of actually treating Black men as criminals, which results in the loss of life, liberty, and the pursuit of happiness for these men. The idea that Black men are expected to be criminal and dangerous in the United States and United Kingdom is known as the criminalblackman construct (Gabbidon et al., 2002). Katheryn Russell-Brown (1998) used the stereotypic myth criminalblackman to describe how people associate young Black men with crime in American culture. She further added that the Black male is portrayed as a "symbolic pillager of all that is good" (Russell-Brown, 1998). This view of Black men results in underemployment and unemployment, increases in health problems, increased rates of incarceration, and often, death.

Social Labeling Theory

Seeing the acts of an individual as dependent upon and connected with society is rooted in philosophy and sociology and the work of Mead (1914, 1955) who focused on symbolic interaction. He saw the self as a social construct. Moreover, he understood the interaction of the self and the mind as a social process. He further developed concepts of the I and the Me. He saw the "me" as the social self and the "I" as the response of an individual to the attitudes of others. He explored how symbolic meaning and language were related to social interactions (Mead, 1914). His philosophy is essential to understanding the influence of society on the individual and their interrelatedness.

Another construct of interest in understanding stereotyping is the Social Labeling Theory first posited by Tannebaum (1938), who took an interdisciplinary and global approach to understanding crime and the community. He explained that crime is a product of the community, that previous theories of crime are but partial, and that crime is a sociological phenomenon and not necessarily a psychological one. He pointed out that many criminal behaviors are caused by the society or are perpetrated by so-called law abiding citizens. He explained that many elected officials are connected with crime and gang members, and that police agencies often condone criminal behavior.

Tannebaum, (1938, p. 5), opposed ideas of criminology that developed out of Rationalism in the 17th and 18th centuries, which held that people commit crimes because of the pleasures resulting from the crimes and that, moreover, the pleasures are more important to the criminal than theological or moral considerations. Tannebaum held that this rationalistic paradigm removed societal culpability for individuals' crimes and erroneously placed the responsibility solely on the perpetrator. An opposing idea to rationalism came from the positive school of criminology, which held that crime is actually the result of society labeling classes of individuals as criminals.

Lemert developed the concept of deviance from a sociological perspective. He described deviance as primary and secondary. Primary deviance occurs before the labeling while secondary deviance is in response to the primary labeling. In this context, criminal behavior is understood as acts that set the individual against society (Lemert, 1951). Lemert further questioned bell-shaped norms and explained that in some circumstances the J shape may be a better descriptor (Lemert, 1951). He seemed to suggest that the process of labeling may cause more criminal behaviors than the deviance did initially.

According to Becker (1963), an outsider is someone who can't be trusted to live by the rules agreed upon by the group. Becker is considered the father of the Social Labeling Theory. He focused on the concept of social deviance and indicated that society places more emphasis on the person than the person's behavior. Becker saw deviance as a social construct. The Social Labeling Theory, also known as the Labeling Theory, explains stereotyping. It basically holds that once a person is labeled, then the person is likely to own that label and perpetuate what that label stands for. He further pointed out that the American criminal justice system targets minorities who, because they are labeled, are more likely to be accosted and prosecuted (Becker, 1963).

Becker (1963) indicated that in America, European Americans determine what normal and deviant behaviors are. He contended that to label someone deviant reinforces the deviant behaviors. In essence, labeling results in self-fulfilling prophecy; that is, a person called a criminal will act like a criminal. The European American bases these prejudices on limited information and stereotypes. Becker (1963) believed that the personal responsibility for deviance may only be applicable in a minority of cases, and that society is most probably responsible for the deviance seen in individuals. This seems to hold society partly culpable for individual crimes. Becker (1963) elaborated on the concept of deviance as it relates to outsiders. He explained that deviance is a relative concept. He gave the example that a Black man who assaults a White woman is will be punished more than a White man who commits the same offense.

Edwin Sutherland is considered the most influential criminologist of the twentieth century. He coined the term white collar crime. His work focused on the social and environmental causes of crime as opposed to the personal and genetic. His work countered the belief that aristocrats and the king can do no wrong (Sutherland, 1949). Becker agreed with Sutherland's analysis, that crimes committed by corporations are mostly prosecuted civilly instead of criminally (Becker, 1963). Becker held that a person needs to commit just one offense to be labeled a criminal. He stated further that a Black person's status as Black is not superseded by his or her wealth or occupation.

Rosenthal and Jacobsen (1966) explored whether telling teachers to expect higher IQs of certain students would affect the IQ score those student would receive. Flannagan's nonverbal IQ Tests of General Ability (TOGA) were administered to all students at an elementary school in the South San Francisco school district. Of the students, 20% were assigned to the experimental group (their teachers were told that they were expected to have higher IQ gains). Eight months later the students were re-administered IQ tests and, as predicted, the students who were expected to have higher IQ gains did in fact receive higher IQ scores. This was called the teacher expectancy.

Moreover, the experimental groups at the lower grades scored significantly higher than students at the higher grades (Rosenthal & Jacobsen, 1966). This study highlights the dangers of labeling. Like stereotypes, a label is a two-edged sword. Not only does it harm and impact the person stereotyped, but it also has an effect on the group of individuals who believe the label/stereotype. It suggests that prejudicial labels can affect not only the person receiving the label but others as well.

Cooley was another pioneer on the topic of social labeling theory. He saw individual change in society as a process (Cooley, 1922). He focused on the interdependent relationships within a society between people and groups. Cooley also coined the concept of the Looking Glass of Self, which purports that the individual sees the self as others see him or her, like a mirror (p. 65). He stressed that pride and shame are products of the individual imagining what effect his or her reflection has on the minds of others. This study is significant because it suggests that when a person is labeled, the label has an effect on the self.

Schur (1965) explained that overzealous legislatures make unnecessary laws that target people who are unjustly deemed by society to be deviants. He explained that these are typically phantom crimes where there are no victims, and that in these cases greater harm is done to the people being labeled as deviant. These laws create a class of deviance and they cause people to develop a deviant self-image; this fosters sub-cultures and creates secondary crimes (crimes that so-called deviants commit in efforts to support their deviant habits that resulted from being called a deviant) (Schur, 1965, p. 171). Regarding labeling, Schur contended that those in power determine who and what is labeled. He explained that the way to address this is through community, social, and civic initiatives that empower those without it (Schur, 1965). Moreover, minorities are at greater risk of accepting their labeling as criminal (Wellford, 1975). Other researchers (i.e., Link, Cullen, Struening, Shrout,

& Dohrenwend, 1989) acknowledge what they consider valid criticism of the Labeling Theory, but add that the criticisms downplay the harm done in labeling. They developed a modified Labeling Theory to better explain the psychological harm done in labeling psychiatric patients. These researchers relied on a study (i.e., Scheff, 1966) that held that once a person is labeled that person is subjected to certain responses from others. One's behaviors then conform to those expectations and are stabilized through rewards and punishments. Then the individual internalizes the community's attitude toward the self in what is called the generalized other. In essence, the identity formed around a mental illness maintains the mental illness. Link and colleagues (1989) modified their Labeling Theory to demonstrate that, in labeling, society is setting in motion a process of discrimination and devaluation that causes coping mechanisms of secrecy and withdrawal. Consequently, the labeled person's self-esteem is harmed, their earning potential decreased, and their social network ties broken.

Social labeling can lead to increases in juvenile delinquency. Adams, Robertson, Gray-Ray, Ray, and Melvin (2003) explored the relationship between negative labels and delinquent behavior. They investigated as well whether teachers and peer groups are important sources of negative labels, which can then lead to the adoption of a deviant self-concept. Several high school juveniles in Mississippi were selected to explore attitudes regarding drugs and delinquent behaviors. These juveniles had been remanded to the custody of Mississippi Youth Services for various offenses. Participants completed two questionnaires, one regarding formal labeling and the other informal labeling. Formal labeling addressed attitudes about feeling labeled as a result of being formally processed through the juvenile system. Informal labeling addressed attitudes about feeling casually labeled, labeling that resulted after being formally labeled. Questions were related to contacts with the police, court proceedings, incarceration, probation, and counseling.

After completing the informal labeling questions, participants were asked to identify the labels that best reflected the perception of them from the perspective of three groups of significant others: parents, teachers, and peers. The descriptive contrasting adjectives were as follows: (a) cooperative or troublesome, (b) good or bad, (c) conforming or deviant, (d) obedient or disobedient, (e) polite or rude, and (f) law-abiding or deviant (Adams et al., 2003).

Results were used to understand the relationship between labeling and negative self-concept and were assessed using a Cronbach's alpha analysis. Moreover, three additional tests were used to assess the impact of delinquency on self-concept: the General Delinquency Index, the Drug-related Delinquency Index, and the Serious Delinquency Index. Findings indicated that teachers were important sources of negative labeling but that negative labeling by social control agents was also important. Results also showed that racial background was not a significant predictor of involvement in drug offenses (Adams et al., 2003). This is significant for understanding whether Black men are more criminal than White men as it relates to drug offenses. Finally, results showed that secondary delinquency is more a function of formal labeling than informal labeling and that labeling in general was a significant predictor of certain types of delinquency (Adams et al., 2003).

MacMaster, Donovan, and MacIntyre (2002) looked at the effects of being labeled as learning disabled on self-esteem. The participants were fifth grade students, 33 with learning disabilities and 36 without learning disabilities. The male-to-female ratio was about equal. The Rosenberg Self-Esteem Inventory was administered to measure self-esteem. It was discovered that the children with learning disabilities had significantly lower self-esteem than the control group initially. At a later time self-esteem was measured again. The self-esteem for the children with learning disabilities increased. This was postulated to be due to the fact that they were probably now comparing themselves to other children with learning disabilities. Self-esteem also increased because they saw the remediation as helping them to improve and that, therefore, their learning disabilities were limited in scope. These results tend to suggest that the perception of the stigma of the label is a significant factor in how one views oneself, and that children with learning disabilities tend to compare themselves with other children with learning disabilities. While the above study appears inconsistent with prior labeling research, the condition of the labeling in this study was one of providing aid. In essence the labels and condition above were for positive purposes, not demonization, and were perceived as such.

Labeling gives a descriptor on the basis of behavior or a physical characteristic; in society, this labeling places people in groups with others having a similar label (Gold & Richards, 2012). Martinez and colleagues (2011) studied whether being labeled mentally or physically ill impacts if a person is viewed less humanely and more dangerously; furthermore, they studied how individuals actually formulate impressions of others when given limited information. In the first part of this study, participants were presented with examples of individuals who were mentally and physically ill and asked to give impressions. The second part of this study selected participants from an email list of a nationwide sample. Of the participants, 96 were women and 78 were men. Ethnicity was represented as follows: 72.6%, Caucasian/White; 17.8%, Asian-American/Pacific Islander; 3.4%, African American; 4.1% Hispanic/Latino; 0.7% Indian/Alaskan Native; and 1.4% declined to state ethnicity.

Results indicated that mental health labels resulted in reduced perception of humanity and increased views that one was dangerous and socially rejected. It was discovered that chronic mental illness triggered perceptions of decreased humanity compared to the chronically physically ill label. Also, the chronically mentally ill label resulted in greater perceived threat, compared to those labeled chronically physically ill.

Gold and Richards (2012) addressed the disproportionate representation of African American boys in special education programs and see this as discrimination. They argued that special education is a labeling system and that the labeling of African American boys in special education is counterproductive. Moreover, the baggage that comes with the label is worse than the benefits received from special educational services. They contended that to say African Americans are unable to learn is discriminatory and promotes deficit thinking, a circumstance that African Americans have had to contend with throughout American history. They also noted that, like general education classrooms, special education classrooms are not culturally competent. In an effort to clarify this point, Obiakor (as cited by Gold & Richard, 2012) indicated that in special education subjects, African-American students who might learn differently because of their cultural influences, risk misidentification, misassessment, misclassification, misplacement, and misinstruction. They suggest that special education is an additional label to many other labels that African Americans have been given.

Metzl's (2010) investigation addressed the social injustices of Black men diagnosed with schizophrenia in the Iona State Prisons in Michigan in the 1960s and 1970s. He was concerned that Black men were stereotyped and mislabeled with schizophrenia. His research consisted of reviewing the prison archives, where he found that Black men were disproportionately misdiagnosed with schizophrenia during the 1960s and 1970s just for protesting the conditions at the Ionia State Prison in Michigan. Moreover, he indicated that discomfort concerning race often influenced the doctor-patient relationship. He noted that since the 1920s schizophrenia was considered a feminine disorder, but that now it was seen as an urban male psychosis, correlated with aggression. Metzl indicated that schizophrenia is found in only 1% of the U.S. population, but that Black men were diagnosed five to seven times more frequently.

He also indicated that the perception of aggression was significantly increased in Black men diagnosed with schizophrenia. Metzl's research is relevant to issues related to stereotyping, labeling, and racial profiling of Black men as criminal. Moreover, his research shows how pervasive this labeling is, even among health professionals and in trusted institutions.

Comparison and Contrast of Stereotypes and the Social Labeling Theory

Stereotypes and social labeling are similar in that they both involve assigning characteristics to another without proof that the assigned characteristics are true. They are similar in that they both involve assessments based on preconceived notions (Schneider, 2005. In essence, both stereotyping and labeling involve prejudging another. They are also similar in that both are umbrellas for various subtypes. They both adversely affect Black males. They both have a rich history with roots in maintaining power, control, and order. Stereotypes and labels both benefit the majority and oppress the minority. They are also similar in that they focus on wrongs or problems experienced by minorities and minority groups. They both involve injustices and systematic microaggressions (Becker, 1963).

The basic difference between the social labeling theory and stereotyping is that social labeling not only looks at the injustice in labeling and stereotyping but also on the effects that labeling and stereotyping have on the person labeled or stereotyped (Becker, 1963). Stereotypes primarily look at the cause of prejudging a group in a certain way; labeling looks at the cause and effect of judging. Labeling focuses on the way the person stereotyped owns the label and acts consistent with the label, which justifies to the labeler that validity of the label. In the literature it appears that stereotypes apply more to groups whereas labels are applied more to individuals. Katz and Braly (1933) viewed stereotypes as cultural representations of a group.

Negative Consequences of Criminal Stereotyping

Decreased employment opportunities and wages.

In 2011, Black men made significantly less money than White men at every educational level. Without a high school diploma, White males averaged $22,219; Black men earned $17,093. White male high school graduates made $35,307 and Black males earned $25,418. With some college but no degree, White males earned $39,888, Black men earned $31,455. With associate degrees, White men earned $47,288 and Black men earned $37,452. At the bachelor's degree level, White men earned $69,611 and Black men earned $50,992. With a master's degree, White men earned $88,427 while Black men earned $64,456 (U. S. Department of Commerce, Census Bureau, 2008).

In March 2014, the unemployment rate for adult Black men, age 20 and older, was twice as high as White men (U.S. Department of Labor, 2014). Blacks have among the highest national poverty rates at 25.8% (McCartney, Bishnaw & Fontenow, 2013). From 2007-2011 in 43 states, including the District of Columbia, the poverty rate for Blacks was at least 20%. In 2009, 37.45% of Black under the age of 18 years old, lived in poverty (Pennsylvania Department of Health, 2013). Thus for Black males, the employment rate, poverty rate, infant birth rate, college enrollment rate, and prison incarceration rate are significantly worse than for White males.

Health problems

Being a victim of racist stereotypes results in stress that contributes to health problems and disease (Dressler, Oths, & Gravlee, 2005). Stress is seen in elevated cortisol levels. More than 200 laboratory studies have demonstrated that the highest cortisol levels were found in people who performed tasks outside of their control that involved what epidemiologist Richard Wilkinson has described as stress negatively impacting changes in body chemistry. In essence, high cortisol levels result from being bossed around. Blacks typically are employed in inferior positions (Longmore, 2013). Blacks have the worst health in America, suffering primarily from diabetes, heart disease, high blood pressure, HIV, and obesity (Feagin & McKinney, 2003).

Fang and Myers (2001) examined the negative consequences that discrimination has on health, quality of life, and life span. They discovered that Black men who were discriminated against, and who consequently held in frustrations, had higher blood pressures. A Black male child is 2.3 times less likely to reach his first birthday and is 80% less likely to reach his fifth birthday than a White child (Longmore, 2013). At 15 years of age, Black males are 60% less likely to reach their 16th birthday than White males. Moreover, Black men who reach the age of 45 are 80% less likely to live long enough to collect Social Security. In 1990, a black Male residing in Harlem had only a 37% chance of reaching age 65 (Longmore, 2013).

Increased incarceration rate and stereotypes of the criminalblackman

In 2008, Black males were 36% of the prison population, while they made up about 13% of the country's population. The prison population was 31% for White males, who make up around 62% of the country's population (Bureau of Justice Statistics, 2009). The reality is that Black men have always been disproportionately incarcerated, even during slavery. In the 1910 census, Black men were already jailed at disproportionately higher numbers. In the 1930s to 1950s Blacks were arrested and imprisoned six times more frequently in comparison to Whites; this disproportionate number of Blacks incarcerated has existed in the U.S. since the turn of the 20th century (Peterson et al., 2006).

Death

The ultimate negative consequence of criminal stereotyping is death, as seen in the Trayvon Martin case. Trayvon Martin was walking to a store in a gated community in Florida and was accosted by a White/ Hispanic neighborhood watchman, George Zimmerman, who followed and eventually shot and killed Trayvon, even after a police dispatch told Mr. Zimmerman to terminate his pursuit. It wasn't until after months of protests that Mr. Zimmerman was even charged and arrested (Farhi, 2012). Moreover, Black men throughout American history have been killed as a result of criminal stereotypes. While not a complete list, some killed were Emmett Till, Medgar Evers, Malice Green, and Martin Luther King Jr. (Christensen, Barlow, & Ford, 2013).

The concept of Black-on-Black crime is pejorative and should be viewed instead as a national health crisis (Khenti, 2013). In his article entitled, Homicide among Young Black Men in Toronto: An Unrecognized Public Health Crisis, Khenti explained that homicide and crime are direct results of racism, poverty, unemployment, income- inequality, and poor quality of life. He added that this causes Black men to seek gangs as a form of employment and dignity. Finally, Khenti (2013) urged the scientific health field to make this a priority of research and to address this as a health crisis, not as a Black-on-Black crime problem in Toronto. While Khenti's study was performed in Canada, it may help in understanding crime and Black men in America.

Sex, Gender, and Violence

Cohen and Harvey (2006) acknowledged that men commit more crimes, are more violent, and are more likely to find themselves involved with the criminal justice system. There were 1,368,886 men and only 101,179 women in the state and federal prisons in 2003; therefore, one can conclude that crime is mostly a phenomenon among men. This may have to do with gender development. Healthy masculinity tends towards autonomy, strength, independence, and freedom, while unhealthy masculinity tends toward alienation, domination, morbid fear of relationship/commitment, and destruction (Cohen & Harvey, 2006).

Some argue that men commit more crimes due to hormones. Males produce more testosterone and are more likely to express their aggression through physical means (Bjorkqvist, 1994). By the age of two, males generally exhibit more physical aggression, and this has been linked to higher levels of testosterone, while females exhibit more non-physical, indirect behavior and verbal aggression (Landsford, 2002). While biological factors traditionally determine sex, gender is determined by society (West & Zimmerman, 1987). Eagly and Beall (2004) contended that gender functions as a social label and is more of a continuum rather than an exclusive categorization. Furthermore, in understanding gender, the postmodern focus includes as many factors as possible to fully appreciate the nature of male and female; it explores public policy questions, family concerns, and whether parents should rear boys and girls alike. Therefore to better understand Black men and crime, it is necessary to understand multiple indicators, not just sex. Messerschmitt (1993) indicated that criminal behavior can be used as a resource when other resources are not available for accomplishing masculinity. Archer (1994, p. 135) added that the greatest trait of masculinity is occupational and monetary success. Kimmel (1996) indicated that the willingness to fight in any given situation is considered maleness. Performing well in violent situations is considered a traditional display of masculinity (Messerschmitt, 1993). If traditional means are not available, then violence is likely to result. Those who have used violence in the past are more likely to use violence in the future (Messerschmitt, 2000). While aggression and physical force are historically characteristic of maleness in resolving conflicts, gender roles are often constructed and not all men have the same amount of masculine traits (Hagedorn, 1998).

Krienert (2003), in exploring the effects of expression of masculinity on violence, tested Messerschmitt's hypothesis of whether those with fewer outlets to express masculinity would commit more crimes. The participants in his study, 1,658 violent and 760 non-violent males, were interviewed in Lincoln, Nebraska. The Masculinity-Femininity scale on the MMPI was used to measure masculinity. In efforts to measure outlets to express masculinity, the following characteristics were explored (happily married, fathering children, and job satisfaction). Results indicated that males who exhibited more masculine traits but had fewer acceptable outlets to assert their masculinity were more likely to be involved in violent events (Krienert, 2003). The above study is relevant to exploring stereotypes associated with Black men as it suggests that the deprivation of the basic needs of life is directly connected with crime as opposed to gender or other traits, such as race.

Men and Emotions

In exploring emotions of men and animals, Charles Darwin concluded that, unlike women, Englishmen rarely cry (Mead, 1955). In comparing the emotions of men and women, Cirillo, Kaplan, and Wapner (1989) reported that women by nature are more nurturing and prone to shame. On the other hand, men are less likely to show shame, even when they feel it. This is part of the evolutionary culture where men are more dominant and women are more caring. Thus men are less likely to show their emotions than women when the emotion is connected to shame.

Robertson, Woodford, Lin, Danos, and Hurst (2001) studied why men have difficulty expressing themselves emotionally. They found that all men, like women, were physiologically aroused by emotion-eliciting stimuli, but men prefer exercise and structured tasks rather than open-ended talk about their inner feelings. Moreover, in the family men would rather do things than become highly invested emotionally. Finally, men have fewer outlets for emotional expression in U.S. culture. While men report fewer emotional responses, they have similar physiological experiences. In essence, all men have physiological similarities, even though some have reported experiencing fewer stressors. The natural emotional experiences of men and women are similar, but men are nurtured to not express emotions at the level women do.

Salovoy and Sultor (1997) found that emotional intelligence is extremely important to a child's development and adaptation. Emotional intelligence is defined as "the ability to perceive emotions, to access and generate emotions so as to assist thought, to understand emotions and emotional knowledge, and to reflectively regulate emotions so as to promote emotional and intellectual growth." (Salovoy & Sultor, 1997, p. 5). Moreover, reasoning that takes emotions into account and emotional development is posited as especially critical to a child's development. It is believed that mood affects thinking in positive or negative ways; therefore, it is important to have a healthy mood.

Emotional development is not just shaped by the family but also by the school peers and society. How one experiences positive affirmation affects emotional development. How does the negative stereotyping that Black men experience in society affect the way they may experience their family? If a child grows up feeling positive about him or herself, then he or she will develop a sense of wellbeing, problem-solving capability, and resilience to deal with problems in life (Salovoy & Sultor, 1997).

Finally, Bly (1990) uses the analogy of Vietnam to describe the fractured emotional bond between fathers and sons. Older leaders in the military sent the younger men into harm's way in Vietnam without going themselves, which resulted in unnecessary deaths and distrust. Likewise fathers often have a fractured relationship with their sons and are not preparing their sons emotionally for life. He indicated that the industrial revolution fractured father/son relations by causing fathers to work next to their sons instead of teaching them face to face. Moreover, the demands of the workplace caused fathers to return home in bad moods, hindering relations with their sons. Competition and rules further interfered with the connection that is necessary for father/son positive relations. Lastly, the work that needs to be done must be done by older men in society, acknowledging younger men for who they are and their contributions. When this emotional connection happens, men will become more nurturing to their own wives and families (Bly, 1990).

Black Men and Emotions

As a result of racism and discrimination while growing up, Black boys see negative messages, primarily in the media, that do not promote success for them, but rather failure and devaluation. This message is first reinforced at home and school from emasculated fathers and a school environment that devalues the Black males (Hooks, 2004). Consequently, the patriarchal socialization that insists boys should not express emotions or be recipients of emotional caretaking is most viciously and ruthlessly implicated in the early childhood socialization of Black boys. The image of emasculated and powerless Black males is so embedded in the cultural imagination that many Black parents feel it is crucial to train boys to be tough. (Hooks, 2004, p. 86)

Shamir and Travis (2002) found that the Black Panther movement in part influenced the Black male identity formation to express fewer emotions and to appear tougher, evidenced by the leather attire and orientation towards self-defense. This emotional defensiveness is ingrained the social identity-formation of Black men. Emotional protectiveness developed in response to the discrimination Blacks encountered, historically and during the civil rights period, which influenced Black nationalist identities. The hardening of emotions in some Black men is caused by the historical oppression whose intent is to destroy Black families (Kunjufu, 1986).

Summary

The process of demonizing Black men as criminals started with the forced migration of Africans to America. Millions of Africans were kidnapped and brought to America to build the infrastructure and wealth of this country. Slavery was not just a problem of the South; the original slaves arrived on the northeastern shores as well. Slavery existed in both the North and the South. Abraham Lincoln originally opposed the ending of slavery but was willing to do whatever was necessary to preserve the Union, even if it involved freeing the slaves.

The idea that Blacks were inferior to Whites was pushed in Germany and the movement swelled across Europe and into America. Whites were considered superior to Blacks and were said to be more intelligent and attractive. These ideas furthered the subjugation of Blacks and justified their mistreatment (Painter, 2010). Viewing Blacks as inferior encouraged Whites to criminalize Blacks. Even when slavery ended with the Emancipation Proclamation and 13th Amendment, there were still efforts to view Blacks as inferior to Whites and to keep them in a place of second class citizenship.

Jim Crow laws were instituted to keep Blacks separate from Whites unless the Blacks were serving Whites in some capacity. Blacks were criminalized for not having employment, even though they were discriminated against in employment. Blacks were forced into sharecropping and often not paid; when they were paid, they were given non-living wages. Often Blacks were falsely accused of crimes and convicted without due process.

The civil rights movement attempted to remove racial discrimination, which included the demonization of Blacks as criminal. The 1866 Civil Rights Act did not have the force of law, so therefore the oppression of Blacks continued (Curry, 1996). After the Civil War, Blacks made gains during Reconstruction. As soon as the federal troops left the South, however, Black Codes and Jim Crow laws were passed to bolster the stereotype of Blacks as inferior and criminal, thus justifying oppression. In America, four thousand seven hundred thirty nine people were lynched between 1882 until the early 1950s (the actual number is about six-thousand); 82% of the lynchings occurred in the South; 84% were Black and 82% were male. Most of the lynchings, five hundred eighty one, occurred in Mississippi, five hundred thirty nine were Black (Painter, 1991).

This chapter has explored the impact of institutional racism on marginalizing Blacks and the consequences of this practice. Chief Justice Warren of the U.S. Supreme Court highlighted how stereotyping of and discrimination against Blacks have been harmful to their self-esteem and are likely to do harm that might never be undone. The 1964 Civil Rights Acts demanded that Blacks be treated equally, humanely, and fairly (Loevy, 1997). The 1965 Voters Rights Act - granted equal rights in voting (Pitts, 2008). Moreover, after the civil rights movement of the 1960s and the Affirmative Action executive order, the Critical Race Theory (CRT) movement started, due to concerns about enforcement and attempts made to reverse gains made in civil rights. CRT theory research addressed concerns about the effects of society and culture on race, law, and power (Yosso, 2006). It saw racism as ingrained in American culture. CRT is concerned that Whites view themselves as superior to Blacks and that they believe that Blacks must be controlled and granted only limited power. The CRT movement produced research and scholarship that addresses the criminalization of Black men in America.

In this chapter stereotypes were explored from the 1920s to the present and their relationship to society, race, and Black men in particular examined. Lippman (1922) indicated that stereotype is a thought about a person that may not be based in reality. He described stereotypes as imagining things before we experience them. This phenomenon was explored relative to research that addresses how vastly stereotypes have been applied to different minority groups in efforts by the majority to maintain power.

Allport (1979) defined race as a social attitude propagated among the public by an exploiting class for the purpose of stigmatizing some group as inferior, so that the exploitation of either the group or its resources may both be justified. Lastly, Correll and colleagues (2007) studied stereotypes as they relate to Black men and criminal behaviors. In interviewing college students at the University of Chicago, they looked at the effects of race on the decision of people to shoot White men and Black men. The exposure to stereotypes regarding Black men as criminal increased the likelihood that Black men would be shot more than White men. Moreover, Jones and Kaplan (2003) used college students to study whether juries were more likely to convict Blacks of stereotypical violent crimes than Whites. Results indicated that Blacks were convicted more than Whites for stereotypical violent crimes.

This chapter also addressed the stereotypic criminalblackman myth and how it is seen in various institutions that either explicitly or implicitly marginalize Black men. The criminalblackman is a myth that perpetuates the stereotype that young Black men are criminal (Russell-Brown, 1998). This myth can be seen in the criminal justice system in the New York stop, question, and frisk cases. This chapter addressed the intellectualization, rationalization, and constitutional implications that illegal searches have on Black men.

This chapter also addressed Social Labeling Theory (Labeling Theory) and how the idea of labeling a Black male as criminal serves as an indictment or self-fulfilling prophecy in seducing Black males to own that stereotype. Becker (1963) indicated that the American criminal justice system targets minorities who are more likely to be arrested and prosecuted.

Drapetomania, the urge to escape felt by slaves, was also addressed as a diagnostic label aimed at justifying oppression of Blacks in the antebellum South. Moreover, this chapter addressed how men were misdiagnosed as schizophrenic after engaging in reasonable protests of prison conditions in Ionia, Michigan in the 1960s and 1970s.

Finally, this chapter explored the negative consequence of criminal stereotypes to Black men such as increases in incarceration rate, multiple health problems, poorer quality of life, and reduced employment wages for Blacks with the same educational qualifications as Whites. But the ultimate adverse consequence of criminal stereotypi6ng is death, as seen in the Trayvon Martin case. This chapter addressed literature that supports the historical oppression of Black people in America and the stereotyping of Black men as criminal. It also addressed efforts to justify White supremacy's impact on Blacks. This chapter focused on how Black men have often been the victims of a culture in America that has stereotyped them as criminalblackmen. This profiling and scrutiny have negatively affected employment and educational opportunities for Black men. As a result, Black men have higher incarceration rates. Finally, this chapter questioned the idea that just because a person is a male he must be more criminal. Krienert (2003) concluded that when a male has more outlets to express his masculinity, he commits fewer crimes.

Chapter III
How to Detect Racial Profiling

The purpose of this chapter is to provide the rationale and theoretical foundation for selecting the qualitative narrative model in explaining the experiences of Black men relative to criminal stereotypes. Also included in this chapter is a brief history of qualitative analysis. Lastly, the methods and procedures used to gather, store, organize, and analyze the data for this study will be reviewed.

Most research describing the psychology of Black men in connection with criminology is based on quantitative statistics. These statistics generally focus on the who and what and leave the why to be explained and interpreted by people other than the Black men described in the statistics. This study examines the experiences of Black men and allows them to explain their experiences relative to criminal stereotypes. This approach is unique but adds to research in this field by explicating the phenomenon of the disproportionate representation of Black men relative to crime.

Constructivist Philosophy

During the 19th century, positivist philosophers indicated that the world was independent of the researcher and that information gained was primarily arrived at through rational means. Positivists also held that the knowledge gained through rational means was free from researcher bias. This was the basis of quantitative analysis as positivists attempted to gain insight into social problems (Taylor & Bogdan, 1998).

Constructivism is the basis upon which qualitative analysis evolved. Constructivist epistemology is based on the assumption that there is no single valid methodology in science but rather a diversity of useful methods. It opposes the philosophy of objectivism. Constructivism is a branch of the philosophy of science where mental constructs are used to explain sensory experiences of the natural world (Crotty, 1998). The philosophy of Constructivism is rooted in Greek philosophy, such as that of Heraclitus, Protagoras, and Plato. Some of the constructs upon which constructivists rely are: metaphysics, what can be factual about the world; epistemology, what can be known about the world; and semantics, what can be said about the world (Kulka, 2000).

Constructivists do not understand scientific research in terms of objective absolutes but rather as theoretical processes constructed by scientists.

Epistemic-relativism, a type of constructivism, suggests that absolute belief depends on culture, the individual, or a paradigm (Kulka, 2000). In explaining an example of how facts are social constructions, Kulka (2000) explained that money is constructed because society gives it its value and anyone disagreeing will be factually mistaken. Likewise, scientific facts are socially constructed before they become fact. Therefore, what is known as objective and scientifically natural cannot be absolutely known, according to Knorr-Cetina (1993), and thus, aspects of science are relatively constructed. Constructivism is a social science perspective that explains what is seen. Nelson (1994) indicated that constructivism is opposed to rationalism, as rationalism makes claims of epistemic absolutism and realism. In exploring the experience of Black men relative to criminal stereotypes, this research focuses is on what their experiences are. By focusing on the what, constructivism paves the way for qualitative research.

Qualitative Research

In conducting qualitative research the researcher often seeks to discover that which is hidden or not told rather than determine whether something is in fact true (Josselson & Lieblich, 1999).

Qualitative research is a means of exploring and understanding the meaning individuals or groups ascribe to social or human problems. This process of research involves emerging questions and procedures. Data is typically collected in the participant's setting, data analysis inductively builds from particulars to general themes, and the researcher makes interpretations of the meaning of the data." (Creswell, 2009, p. 4)

The data in qualitative analysis is actually the participants' expressions of their experiences (Marshall & Rossman, 2006).

Qualitative research relies on multiple sources, such as observations, interviews, and documents, rather than a single data source. Moreover, qualitative research uses deductive research, building from the bottom up (Creswell, 2009).

Moustakas (1990) indicated that qualitative research is descriptive in nature, using words, writings, films, recordings, and behaviors. The aim of qualitative research is to understand a social situation, event, role, group, or interaction (Locke, Spirduso, & Silverman, 2000). "It's an investigatory process where the researcher gradually makes sense of the social phenomenon by contrasting, comparing, replicating, cataloging and classifying the object of study" (Creswell, 2009, p. 194). During the qualitative process, the researcher is involved in face-to-face encounters with the participant where data is collected.

Qualitative research is not based on mathematics but focuses on descriptive data and is non-statistical (Strauss & Corbin, 1998). While the quantitative researcher starts with a hypothesis and sets out to examine it (Falk & Blumenreich, 2005), qualitative research starts with indefinite questions that determine the methodology (Taylor & Bogdan, 1998). Quantitative research focuses on causation and correlation to arrive at meaning. The narrative model comes from a qualitative research perspective.

Narrative Research Model

The narrative research model is one of many qualitative models and is rooted in anthropology, sociology, and feminism (Webster & Mertova, 2007). It was developed in the postmodern 20th century. Narrative research is a strategy of inquiry in which the researcher studies the lives of individuals and asks one or more individuals to provide stories about their lives. Pokinghorne (1995) first introduced the narrative model to psychology in efforts to better understand the experiences of humans (Clandinin, 2007). The goal in the narrative model is to understand and create meaning from the participants' lived experiences. This information is often then retold or re-storied by the researcher in a narrative chronology. In the end, "the narrative combines views from the participant's life with those of the researcher's life in a collaborative narrative" (Creswell, 2009, p. 4). Narrative research involves a re-storytelling of the participant's story using structural devices, such as plot, setting, activities, climax, and denouement (Clandinin & Connelly, 2004).

A person's life experience is the basis of the narrative that is relived throughout the interview process. This source of information is examined and collected (Webster & Mertova, 2007). Human phenomena and the meaning people give to their own lives are explored. This type of research is not interested in the meaning that non-participants give to the participants' lives (Etherington, 2004). As a research participant, the interviewer is an active part of the process. Verbal and nonverbal gestures and the conduct of the interviewer affect the interview process, in terms of what is said, how it is said, and how it is recorded and interpreted (Clandinin & Connelly, 2000). It is therefore important for the researcher to be aware of his/her impact on the participant and the process.

In using the narrative model to explore the experience of African American men relative to criminal stereotypes, the goal was to focus more on what was said, or the structures of what was said, to gain greater social meaning out of the stories (Bleakly, 2005). The narrative model appears well suited to unpack the experiences of Black men relative to criminal stereotypes. In using this model, it is hoped that themes from unique experiences will be located.

The narrative model focuses on the contexts in which narratives are constructed. It addresses the nature of the person telling the narrative, the context from which the narrative is created, the relationships between the narrative teller and others within the narrative, historical continuity, and the chronological organization of events. A beginning, middle, and end are constructed from the narrative data.

Polkinghorne (1995) makes the distinction between narrative analysis and analysis of narratives. He explains that narrative analysis focuses on shaping data into stories such that each participant has his/her own narrative. Analysis of narratives focuses on identifying and analyzing themes and shaping narrative stories from the themes.

Narrative stories are important not only because they provide a wealth of knowledge and understanding about people and their experience but because they also affect others, society, opinions, and views (Bruner, 1990). Therefore, in addition to understanding the participants and their experiences and the impact their experiences have on them, conducting narrative research impacts society and others.

Methods and Procedures

This section describes how the researcher prepared for collecting the data. It includes the criteria for selecting research participants; a plan that ensured confidentiality; and the location, length, frequency, and documentation of the interviews. This section also describes the plan for conducting the interviews and the plan for handling, organizing, and analyzing the data.

Collecting Data

After approval was granted from the institutional review board (IRB), participants were recruited by posting fliers in community colleges, churches, and universities utilizing the snowballing method. Twelve participants in the study met the following criteria: they were Black males age 18 or older with citizenship or at least a 10-year history of having lived in the U.S. prior to entering college, and they had experienced being stereotyped as a criminal. Each participant was required to read and sign an informed consent agreement. They were given a Letter of Introduction that introduced them to the researcher and informed them of the researcher's background and contact information. Before the interviews started, participants were informed of the possible risks and benefits of participating in the study and told that they could discontinue the study at any point during the interview. Participants were required to use pseudonyms to protect their privacy. The interviews used open-ended questions. Participants were also provided with an opportunity to be put in touch with a counselor if needed. After the interviews were completed, the audio recordings were transcribed.

Organizing and Analyzing the Data

The first stage was reading the data. Etherington (2007) explained that there is no set way of organizing narrative data, and that flexibility is allowed for the researcher. In this study, all data collected via an audio voice recorder was transferred to digital audio files that were stored on a computer and transcribed. All digital recordings will be deleted seven years after this dissertation is completed. In starting the analysis, the 12 transcripts were read for general understanding and meaning. The narrative method allows great flexibility in analyzing the meaning of participants' lived experiences. The story should be understood within the greater context of the individual's current experience (Maple & Edwards, 2010). After reading the transcripts, they were conceptualized in light of participants' present experiences. This initial reading provided an overview of general themes and ideals. It elicited awe, wonder, humor, and concerns but mostly a desire to delve more deeply to understand more.

The second process was constant comparison analysis which included the researcher first reading through the entire set of data. Then the data was extracted and categorized into smaller meaningful parts. Then each grouping was labeled with a descriptive title or a "code." The researcher then compared each coded grouping with previous codes, so similar groupings would be labeled with the same code. After all the data had been coded, the codes were grouped by similarity and a theme was identified and documented based on each grouping (Onwuegbuzie & Leech, 2007). Highlighters of different colors were used to mark themes and subthemes. By this re-storying, experiences of Black men relative to criminal stereotypes emerged.

Thirdly, transcripts were re-read several times. This is called the explication phase, the period of focusing on themes for greater meaning. Clandinin and Connelly (2000) indicated that stories should be read over and over again for understanding meaning and social significance in order to shape all data into a research text. Through this process, themes began to emerge concerning the experiences of Black men relative to criminal stereotypes. Throughout the re-storying process, major themes that were common for all participants were highlighted with certain colors. For instance, Theme 1 was highlighted red for all participants, Theme 2 was highlighted blue for all participants, and so on. Subthemes were then identified and likewise received different highlighted colors.

Criteria for Selecting Themes

To develop themes, attention was focused on what participants emphasized most and what was uniform or common. After going over the stories multiple times, certain points or ideas stood out and were consistent for participants. Secondly, themes were narrowed using a cross analysis method found in consensual qualitative research (CQR). This is a process that identifies frequencies of categories across participants (Hill, Thompson, & Williams, 1997). Frequency categories include general, all but one; typical, more than half and up to the general cut-off; variant, up to two cases, up to the cutoff of typical; and rare, two to three cases (Hill, 1997). This process was checked several times for accuracy. Through this narratology, themes and subthemes emerged. To determine subthemes the same process was used but the frequency was seen by less than or equal to half of the participants. The goal in this process is not so much whether these stories were told but whether they were heard (Cortazzi, 1993).

Nonverbal Data

In addition to verbal expressions, the narrative model assesses for non-verbal emotions and behavioral expressions. It also allows participants' perceived expressions of emotions and non-verbal behaviors to be collected as a part of the narrative (Manusov, 2005). Collecting nonverbal data is essential to this study of the experience of Black men relative to criminal stereotypes because Black men often do not verbalize trauma or victimization (Hooks, 2004).

Nonverbal data is essential for obtaining deeper meanings of a contextual nature of the participants' experience. Moreover, facial expressions and hand gestures clarify the meaning of words (Kelly, Barr, Church, & Lynch, 1999). Communication involves more than just words; thus, nonverbal communication is an additional method of obtaining data (Bull, 2001).

Reflexivity

Reflexivity is the process of involving the self in the research process. Clark Moustakas was the pioneer of this idea and developed it into what is known as heuristic research (Moustakas, 1975, 1990). Etherington (2007) indicated that reflexivity is a skill that we develop as counselors: an ability to notice our responses to the world around us, as well as other people and events, and to use that knowledge to inform our actions, communications, and understandings. In reflexivity, the researcher's story is encouraged in part to reveal values and beliefs that can influence outcomes (Derrida, 1981).

Reflexivity is a method of systematically better understanding complex data and considering the framework upon with it was constructed, including the social context, and reflecting on the data (Alvesson, 2007). Reflexivity relies on the idea that human are reflective and tries to improve the validity of the analysis by improving the relationship between what is examined and the statement made about that which is examined (Alvesson, 2007).

Summary

In this chapter an overview of the philosophical and historical foundations of qualitative research was provided. Secondly, the basis of narrative research was addressed and the approaches used for the organization and analysis of this research's data were presented. The method for conducting narrative research and the relevance of the narrative model to the experience of Black men relative to criminal stereotypes were explained. Lastly, the methods and procedures for the preparation, collection, and the analyzing of the research data were given. The next chapter includes the presentation of the findings of this study. It is hoped that the stories of participants will aid in understanding the psychological and other implications of stereotyping Black men as criminal.

Chapter IV

Hand's Up: Real Life Experience of Racial Profiling

In addressing the riots of the 1960s, King quoted Victor Hugo stating, "If a soul is left in darkness, sins will be committed. The guilty one is not he who sins, but he who created the darkness."

In this chapter, the research findings are presented using narrative methodology. First, 12 of the participants will be briefly introduced. This introduction of the participants provides a snapshot view of their dynamic backgrounds and unique experiences, even though many of their experiences were very similar. Their stories will then be told in more detailed narrative form while respecting and attempting to preserve the individuality of each voice. The four themes and subthemes that emerged among the 12 individual interviews will then be presented.

Dr. Demetrius E. Ford Ph. D. J.D., Psy.D.

Demographic Descriptions and Narratives of Participants

Matt is a 22-year-old, engaged, African American male. He is a meek young man who has a high school diploma and desires to enter a police academy to become a police officer. He works part-time at a home improvement retail store. He's also in training to become a Christian minister. Matt is timid about relating to the police and other authority figures. What is striking is that his frustration and negative encounters with authority and the police causes him to desire to be in a position where he can serve his community as a peace officer with respect for the citizens.

Matt received his high school diploma but did not attend college. Instead he chose to work in order to meet financial needs. He comes from a family of the working poor class. Matt has worked several minimum wage jobs and has found it difficult to advance. He often has felt marginalized and unappreciated. He indicated that at one job, after making an exchange, he was accused of pocketing the money. He indicated that he was not given the chance to explain himself but was told what they believed he'd done. Matt explained that because he knew he was innocent he was so angered by the accusation that he just took off his badge, walked out, and never returned.

Matt indicated that in most jobs he has found it difficult to earn more than minimum wage. He indicated that often the supervisors viewed him with hostility for no apparent reason. Matt indicated that he always tried to work with his supervisors and always was willing to do extra and work overtime if needed. Matt is a quiet-spoken, meek young man and is easy to get along with. He's articulate and dresses neatly. Yet Matt has had a difficult time with building reasonable employment security.

Matt indicated that once he had a job at a factory. He saw an employee smoking and he attempted to smoke but was swiftly corrected. He mentioned how he was confronted aggressively by a White supervisor in public, and that he was so offended that he immediately quit that job too. Matt, although a young man of 22 years, has found little support from his supervisors at work. He indicated that they all were White, he always felt like an outsider, and he was viewed negatively and treated with hostility.

Matt once worked for Kroger and indicated that he always drove there the same way and was often followed by White police officers. He said that the police knew that he worked at Kroger but still followed him. Matt told of one time when a policeman gave him a ticket after accusing him of a traffic violation that never happened. The police officer then told him that if he did not show up for court that the police officer would pick him up and take him to court.

While Matt came from a working poor family, his family was very supportive and loving. Higher education was not an immediate value for Matt, but Matt decided that he wanted to become a police officer. His desire to become a police officer is fueled by his wish to demonstrate the proper way that authority should be exercised as a peace officer. Because Matt is still relatively young, he is not so traumatized by negative experiences with police officers that he doesn't like police officers.

Matt has a barrier to becoming a police officer. As a result of being unfairly treated by police officers, Matt has accumulated tickets that must be paid to clear his license before he can enter the police academy. He does not have enough money to pay the tickets, so for now his future is on hold.

Dan is a 21-year-old, single, African American male. He grew up in a single mother household in poverty in Detroit. He indicated that his family moved often and he developed dust allergies brought on by chronic moving to different residences. He also indicated that he had problems concentrating and struggled academically in school. Because of the struggle for survival, high school did not seem very relevant to Dan. He indicated that he was more attracted to street life because it provided financial assistance that his family needed to survive. He also indicated that he had difficulty identifying with history in school because the people in the books were White and not reflective of his ethnicity.

His mother worked several jobs. He had difficulties concentrating and academic problems. Dan's self-esteem was lowered because of poverty and his inability to have clothing others students were able to purchase. This caused him to withdraw socially. He indicated that his family moved to Atlanta. In Atlanta he was arrested by the police but indicated that he did not spend time in jail. He spoke of how often the police harassed him and his friend when they were doing nothing wrong. On another occasion, he and a few friends were stopped by the police who said they allegedly matched a description and appeared to be doing something suspicious in the car. They were allowed to go without a ticket. On another occasion he was riding in the back seat and was falsely accused of switching lanes without using a signal and ticketed; Dan was in the back seat.

Having attended a southern state university where he majored in history, he reports enjoying learning and sharing information about American History. Although he dropped out, he plans to return. In general, he enjoys sharing information with others and engaging in philosophical discussion. Dan tells how he has been followed around in stores and feels that he is unjustly seen as a hoodlum when he is not. Dan feels he has been singled out and picked on. He feels this is wrong but that he is powerless to change it. He specifically recalled being followed around in a dollar store by the Arab-American who owned the store. He was followed around again while at college in Alabama at a Macy's store. Dan dropped out of college after two years. He lost faith in the system. He saw the education system as not profitable and of no benefit to Blacks. He saw learning a trade as a viable option where he could achieve some success.

Dev is a 31-year-old, single, African American male. His birth parents used drugs and he was adopted at age 4 years of age. He continued to be negatively influenced by extended family members. He also described part of his culture as Asiatic. Dev had a traumatic upbringing as a result of poverty and associating with negative peers in efforts to improve his standard of living. Consequently, he spent time in prison. As an adult, he continued to be subjected to poverty after being released from prison. He was forced to reside in poor neighborhoods and found little assistance from the employment sector.

Dev also developed a distrust of the police brought about by negative and traumatic experiences with them. Once while residing in Kalamazoo, Michigan, he had a problem with his roommate's boyfriend and called the police for assistance. When the police arrived they refused to ask the visitor to leave. After the police left, Dev was assaulted by the visitor. When the police returned, Dev showed the police an injury but the police refused to arrest or ask the visitor to leave, stating that there were different stories. Dev directed the policeman's attention to the injury but the policeman still refused to make an arrest.

Dev's trauma and distrust for the justice system grew deeper when he was charged by the police for possession of a firearm. He indicated that he was subsequently prosecuted under a Safe Neighborhood statute. He claims that he was railroaded. His co-defendants only served six months, while Dev served seven years, four months, and five days, even though his past record was equivalent to that of the co-defendants. Dev told how he was prosecuted federally and not by the state because he was Black.

Dev had additional experiences where he was profiled by the police. He indicated that he was once pulled over allegedly because a rear light was out. When Dev looked the tail light was on. But the police had time to stop and question him, then he was released without a ticket. As a result, he feels that racial profiling is by design. Dev reflected on his incarceration saying that criminal justice is not about rehabilitation or correction but solely punishment.

Due to poverty, incarceration, and being a convicted felon, Dev's earning capacity was ruined. His daughter's mother separated from him and he struggled to provide and maintain visits with his child. Consequently, he developed a distrust of the American dream. He became convinced that he needed to seek additional information about who he was in the hope that he and others like him could obtain equal rights and a chance for success in America.

Dev states that America does not want to help Black men become successful. He indicated that the support system is just not there. Dev indicated that what has kept him from returning to jail is his involvement in the community. He is an active member of a community organization whose goals are to empower Black men toward success. He's involved in mentoring, educating, tutoring, and encouraging Black men to achieve self-empowerment.

Finally, he described his culture as Asiatic. He is still readjusting to community life. He sees himself as a "family man" and a person of philosophical bent, describing himself as I am you. He indicated that he has endured many trials and tribulations. His experiences in jail have caused him to appreciate life more and have contributed to his commitment to mentor young men.

{ BV is a 52-year-old, single, African American man. He states,

> I had a father who was an alcoholic and a mother who worked all day. My father would come home and drink and start arguing and screaming and talking crazy to the kids. It wasn't a normal lifestyle for me growing up. I didn't get too much help with school

from my father because he was always drunk.

BV indicated that he associated with negative peers in effort to earn money. He sold drugs and was incarcerated and developed a criminal record.

As a result of poverty and a poor education, BV found his employment options limited. He dropped out of school at age 16 years of age and took a job at a liquor store. BV experienced a lot of trauma and emotional problems trying to survive on the streets. He was shot in the leg with an AK 47 on a mistaken identity drug case. This left him with a permanent limp.

BV reported multiple instances of police brutality and racial profiling. He indicated that on one occasion as he jay-walked at the same time as a White woman, the police gave only him a ticket. He questioned the police as to why the White woman didn't receive a ticket and the police told him, "I got you and not her." He indicated that on another occasion as he exited a bus, he was accused of trying to steal a car. Most of BV's encounters with police officers were in the city and most police officers he encountered were Black. In Detroit, it seemed that Black officers often took the lead in interrogations and arrests. BV indicated that often White police officers treated him better that Black officers. On one occasion BV resided in an apartment building where there was heavy drug traffic. He was falsely accused by a Black police officer and his head was pushed into a vending machine. The White officer told the Black officer to let him go.

BV was diagnosed with a thought disorder in early adulthood and placed on multiple different psychotropic medications. He has been in and out of various psychiatric institutions. His adaptive functioning is mostly normal, and he is stabilized on medication and has not been re-hospitalized in a long time.

C is a 44-year-old, married, African American male. He reported having a positive childhood and was raised by both parents in a working class family. While he did not attend college, he has maintained constant employment at the same company since graduating from high school. He makes lower middle class wages and is still working. Because of his strong family background, he has been able to deflect but not destroy racism in his environment. He is a Republican and a Christian.

C indicated that he has had a few run-ins with the police where he felt discriminated against. As a teenager, he was riding as a passenger when police traveling in the opposite direction made a U-turn and stopped his car for speeding. He denied they were speeding and was offended by the harassment. In early adulthood he was also shot in the leg after being in the wrong place at the wrong time. He was not happy with how the police responded to the incident, as the police thought he was somehow involved.

C is a deacon at his church and his faith has allowed him to transcend feeling oppressed by racism or racial profiling. C is committed to his faith and family. He is also a professional photographer.

Cal is a 51-year-old, married, African American male. He is a Christian minister and employed as a housekeeper for a business in metropolitan Detroit. He has a huge heart. Actively engaged in his community, he is dedicated to empowering other people. He prides himself on being a person who believes in praying for others, even if they don't pray for themselves. He is a very spiritual person.

Cal struggled throughout his career to maintain a living wage. He was employed with several different companies but still was not able to make much more than minimum wage earnings. As a teenager he visited the South and ran into White children coming from the opposite direction on the same sidewalk. After there was almost a collision, Cal and his associates were stopped by White police officers who told them to get off the sidewalk when approached by Whites. He indicated that he was angered by this experience.

Cal indicated that he was also accosted by the police for wearing a golf hat because they thought he was in a gang. Two years ago, Cal was also unjustly stopped by the police. The police informed him and others in the vehicle that they were looking for someone who was stealing vehicles. Cal indicated that no one in his vehicle met the description and they were allowed to leave without a ticket. Cal indicated that this experience offended him and that after this he had negative feelings toward the police. Cal continues to struggle with poverty although he is employed full- time. He indicated that he has been overlooked for promotions at work. Consequently he sometime feels that his manhood is challenged. This is sometimes a source of distress. He's a licensed minister at his local church and has a strong faith. He balances the frustration he experiences through being marginalized in society with hope and faith.

V is a 47-year-old, married, African American male. He grew up with a single mother and two sisters in Detroit. V had a difficult childhood financially. He was raised by a single mother with two siblings. Eventually, his family was able to move out of the city of Detroit. In their new neighborhood, V indicated that he was called the N word. He reported being followed by the police. He also spoke of how often, while in a retail store, he has been followed around. Once in a gas station he was followed and watched by an Arab American. V indicated that he also experienced racial discrimination from the police in the region of 8 Mile Road.

V is currently unemployed but owns a home and is renting another. His income is low but his family has enough to get by. One of his strengths is that he is a gifted singer. V sings at his local church in Detroit. He is also a handyman and has desires to clean up the city of Detroit, block by block. The experience of poverty and discrimination seems to have affected V's self-esteem. However he continues to strive to improve himself. He was able to develop skilled trade expertise and become a handyman. V is currently married and struggles financially to maintain his household. He was able to purchase his home with his wife and is repairing another home to rent out. His income is low; therefore, he struggles to make ends meet. He also has several children and makes every effort to provide for them.

V indicated that most of his life has been a struggle but his faith gives him the strength to persevere. He is a talented singer and uses his voice to uplift and empower others. Moreover, he feels committed to his neighbors in the city of Detroit. As a way of giving back, he wants to fix up his neighborhood by cleaning up the blight and restarting a block club to empower youth.

Ark is a 34-year-old, single, African American male. He grew up in Detroit and attended the Detroit Public Schools. He resided with his mother who was a school teacher. He indicated that his childhood up to age 13 was positive. He was attracted to the street life and indicated that he did not have an older brother and his father was not around. He is self-employed as a barber. He indicated that he spent nine years in prison. Ark considers himself successful, although he indicated that he spent unnecessary years in prison due to racism. He suggests that he did not have appropriate male mentors and role models in his life to steer him away from negative peer influences who caused him to take risks and enter the criminal justice system.

Ark's experience within prison would not have been as long or traumatic if it wasn't for the racism he experienced there. He stated,

> I was there in the Detention Center and then I got some mail, and it was a bill from a video place. They sent me a bill, then the White guy said, "Dang, you already locked up and you getting

bills." So then I said: "Stay out of mines." then he said: "Nigga, I'll kill you." Then I looked at the corrections officer (a White boy red-neck) and he was like looking like, "You not goin' do nothing." So, I went and threw on my boots and I beat his ass. And through me beating his ass, like I said, they made an example out of me and gave me five years.

Ark seemed to be hardened by the prison experience. When he was released, he committed home invasions. Eventually, Ark turned it around and realized that he needed to be reeducated about how to live in America. He realized that he had been institutionalized and hardened by racism and the prison experience. Ark has ventured on a new path of reeducating others to avoid the traps of poverty and incarceration.

J is a 58-year-old, single, African American male. He was a very successful television personality and won many awards. He said that because of institutional racism that program was discontinued. Due to economic conditions, he experienced financial difficulties. He then pursued employment giving motivational speeches, empowering young Black males to stay off drugs and out of jail. J found a new career path in business but is presently trying to reboot his career as an active civil rights leader and television/radio personality.

R is a 63-year-old, widowed, African American male. R was born and raised in Detroit. He attended the Detroit Public Schools. His father was a licensed electrician. R indicated that he experienced a lot of discrimination, telling how once a man touched his head saying that if he touched a curly boy's head he would have good luck. So he rubbed his hands through his head. On another occasion, R told the story of how one day he rode his bike to Dearborn and was given shredded paper by a stranger. When he asked about that why he was given the paper, the person told him that he was giving it him because no one would ever give him anything in life. R indicated that he was confused again.

R continued to excel educationally but came face to face with racism. Once on an elevator he saw a White woman clutch her purse. He indicated that he has been stopped several times for no apparent reason. He stated,

> I remember one guy declared that my car was stolen. I'm like, so they're going all through my car, looking through this and that. Opening the trunk, you know, in and out, just looking for stuff. I didn't have anything. And I remember I was really irked but it was like I'm all of five eight, 135 pounds, there wasn't too much I could do other than just deal with it.

R was determined to be successful and achieve the American dream. He went to college and received bachelor's, master's and doctorate degrees. He had a major loss in his family that was extremely difficult emotionally to endure; however, he has returned to work and is giving back to the community through his professional services. R indicated that he had struggled in developing his self-identity as a Black male as a consequence of trying to fit in and to live the American dream. Eventually, he was able to receive his doctorate degree and works in the Detroit area.

S is a 33-year-old, single, African American, male. He was born in Germany. S's father was in the military and S traveled all over the world with his father and family. He indicated that he was exposed to different cultures and has learned a lot about diversity. He described himself as a military brat. He indicated that his family lived in Detroit and Colorado. He also indicated that his mother was very religious but had a bad habit that he declined to disclose. He indicated that he was forced to read the Bible and pray as a youth.

S indicated that he was a military child. In Colorado, S faced many challenges at home and indicated that his stepfather physically abused him. There he was involved in several fights with other Whites.

Consequently, his mother sent him to Detroit to reside with his father. He described his father as a street dude. S experienced the challenges of being separated from his mother, separated from his home and school in Colorado. He recounted negative memories of discrimination in Colorado, beatings by his mother, and adjusting to his father's street life.

S recalled that the first thing his father did was to take him to get a haircut and clothes. One morning at 3 a.m., S indicated that his father woke him up and made him fight another boy of similar age. There was money that was being wagered as if they were dogs. He recalled his father training him to get that money. Hustle and kill them Niggas. S indicated that he was being raised by a street father and he wasn't to go back to Colorado. He said that his father taught him how to survive in the hood. This was a cultural shock for him.

S explained surviving in Detroit as follows,

> Like I said, you know the first experience was in Colorado Springs, so it was like you got that proper talk. But here in Detroit, it was like you're gay, "you got that proper talk," you know. I had to go through that phase, so like you gay, you're not their background. My pops, you know, like, humans like you got to have like a certain mentality. But then in my mind, I was thinking, I really don't want to hurt people. Physically, I was more in tune to fucking a person up. So when I went to school I would get teased a lot, you know what it was like— they would say: "Look at how he talk, aw, he gay." Then my pops would say, "You can't keep avoiding all these individuals, you got to go for what you know." Then he was, "We gonna go to this school, I'm a put you in a circle, and either you gone fight, you got to whoop some ass, or you gone get your ass kicked." Then that took me into the egotistical mindset that I just got to be a big bad ass. So going through school I was more of the joke, I want stuff to be

> fun, I would be like a comedian. Sowhen all else failed, when the funny shit don't work, then I got to get on some violence, be a hood nigga, get yo' money. I was taught that that's the only thing that will work with the violence, in Detroit that's it.

S indicated that after high school he enrolled in the military where he learned who he really was and what he preferred without the influence of his parents. He also experienced discrimination in the military, although he wasn't always discriminated against. He was a very good boxer in the military and earned a reputation for being undefeated. Once he was accused of saying negative things about White military officers who were passing by. The officer who was in plain clothes was an MP. He asked to see S's identification and S. replied, "You ain't seeing shit." After the undercover MP persisted, S said "I'm going to knock someone out." At that point he was threatened with arrest by two MPs and charged with instigating a riot and not complying with military police. As a result he lost his status as a boxer. Eventually charges were dropped. S later learned that the undercover MP who instigated the confrontation was the next person S was scheduled to box, but that event was cancelled. S indicated that he felt discriminated against and that it bothered him psychologically.

While still in the military, S. helped a friend retrieve some property from someone who owed him money. S was arrested and interrogated. During the interrogation process, it so happened that S had a tattoo like the person he assisted who was Jamaican. S indicated that one of the MPs stated, "We already know all ya'll some gang-banging porch monkeys." S then responded "Well, if that was the case, we learned it from ya'll, because ya'll just like the Grand Wizards of like the KKK."

S went on to insightfully describe part of his identity formation by stating,

> Ninety percent of Black men who want to be police officers are dealing with an ego trip. They want to feel like they got to have

some power. I don't need nobody to tell me I can have power. I don't need the White man to give me a badge or gun to say 'Here, you got power.' I don't need even a gun to feel like I have power. See, to me, a Black police officer is just a further stage or growth/development of a dope dealer or average street thug. What I mean is it's not the business that they do that gives them the feeling – it's the false feeling of power.

Deo is a 23-year-old, single, African American male. He is unemployed and has difficulties finding work. He detailed that he has several tickets from past traffic violations and has not been able to pay them due to poverty. Deo completed his high school equivalency in Detroit and completed a certificate program as a massage therapist. He indicated that he has had several encounters with the police and feels trapped by the criminal justice system.

Deo's experience is a classic case of racial profiling and the effects of racial profiling on identity formation. Raised in a single-mother-headed family in poverty, his mother also was challenged with mental health problems and took psychotropic medication. Deo struggled with self-esteem issues and security. In efforts to feel more secure and masculine, he associated with negative peers. He was racially profiled on multiple occasions. On one occasion he and his friend were stopped by the police in a White community and told to sit on the ground while it was raining. One of his friends was hit when he questioned the police. They were let go without a ticket.

As a result of poverty and negative experiences with society, Deo developed a dislike for the police and is sensitive to criticism from authority figures. He developed a criminal record, mostly from unpaid tickets from traffic violations. He also developed alcohol/marijuana use problems to self-medicate negative emotions and anxiety. He has been to court several times and feels the justice system was unfair to him on every occasion and did not give him a break or the benefit of the doubt.

While Deo had several disadvantages in his childhood, he also had the positive support of relatives who served as surrogate fathers and mentors. Moreover, his family church has been a place where he could go when he felt despondent. He's currently working full time at a low wage job. While it is not enough for him to move out of poverty, it gives him a sense of pride and allows him to survive.

Themes

Themes were narrowed using both constant comparative analysis and a cross analysis method found in consensual qualitative research, as discussed in the previous chapter.

In this section, the qualities and essence of the experiences of being stereotyped as a criminalblackman are reflected in the collection of themes and subthemes gathered from the data provided by the participants. It is important to note that despite the existence of specific themes there is a certain amount of overlap, due to the nature of the events experienced by the participants. This makes it difficult to completely separate out themes without distorting the continuity and context of the experiences.

During the analysis of the data, four themes and four subthemes emerged. As these themes were synthesized, the experiences of the participants were maintained as their stories were told. The following themes and subthemes arose from the participants' interviews:

1. Racial Profiling
    a) Feeling criminally stereotyped by people in authority
2. Mental Trauma
    a) Fear
    b) Distrust

3. Anger
4. Poverty
    a) Feeling the American dream is a lie

The following section consists of verbatim statements assembled from interviews with various co-researchers that illustrate the common themes and subthemes.

Racial profiling

All of the participants discussed experiences of being approached and aggressively accosted by the police on the basis of their race and being viewed as either having committed a crime or being in the process of committing one. These encounters were unwarranted and without justification. Participants felt their stops were not based on their criminal activity but on ethnic stereotypes.

C recalled an incident in high school of being followed while riding with friends in a car:

> We were going down Van Dyke and a police car was across the street. They were traveling northbound, we were traveling southbound, three to four or five lanes difference between us. There were three of us in the car. They turned around and pulled us over.

Dan recalled an incident of being followed in a store:

> Yeah. I have been followed around in stores. I have been with people that just think I'm from the hood. I'm just a hoodlum, another average kid, just because of the way I dress.

Dan told of another experience of being stopped by the police on the basis of meeting a so-called description:

> Me and a couple friends of mine, we just happened to be riding on the south side of Atlanta one day. We got stopped by two cops, based on a description; they were riding behind us, and said that it seemed like we were doing something suspicious.

Cal indicated that he was stopped two years ago for no apparent reason by the police:

> They told me that people were stealing cars, and they wanted to make sure I was not one of those persons. They also searched me.

J identified a recent experience of being stopped while shopping and interrogated in an aggressive fashion. He reported having been shaken by the experience:

I went to a Meijer store out in West Bloomfield. Meijer is similar to a Wal-Mart. And I'm in there buying my few little things and I'm doing that self-serve, checkout thing that they do now, and I'm not out the door yet, and I hear the cashier, and I see down at one end of the store these two Oakland County cops, White cops, busting out the exit and start running through the parking lot. And I hear one of the clerks, the checkout clerks say, oh they're after somebody now! I though yeah, okay. So I take my stuff and I walk out to my car, my car's down here and these cops are running up here. And the next thing I know, "What's in the bag?" I said, "What do you mean what's in the bag?" He's trying to reach for the bag and I say, "What?" He says, "Well you match the description." I said, "What description?" I said, "What is this, racial profiling?" And we got into it right there because he was . . . so anyway, long story short, there was a man who, a Black man in the store besides me, I guess, who was trying to do something in the prescriptions. Supposedly he was doing a prescription fraud thing. And the description that they gave the cops was a Black man, white shirt. I had on a cream colored yellow shirt. He was not White. He was a Black man. It's got to be him.

J had a unique experience in which he was unjustly confronted by a police officer in a verbally aggressive way that resulted in his incarceration:

> I got accosted by a policeman in Milwaukee because he didn't like my girlfriend's ethnicity. So he began to shout ethnic slurs and I began to shout curse words and I got arrested and I spent the night, or the weekend, in jail. It was the N word.

C spoke on why he thought that the police actually stopped them:

> He saw that three black males were in the car.

Dev addressed a situation where he was not being followed but where he felt mistreated because of his race:

> Me and the codefendant, however, his case remained in the state court. He served six months for the same thing. I served eight years, four months and five days.

Ark also addressed a situation where he was not being followed but where he felt he was mistreated because of his race:

> I meant, I may be walking up the street, minding my own business, or standing on the corner in my own community, and get told to get off the corner by the police.

BV addressed what life was like growing up:

Being an African American male, I find growing up, as a kid there was always a Black and White issue.

BV described an incident where he was stopped by a Black police officer:

> Well, one time, yeah, I was downtown crossing the street. It was a red light. The Black officer asked me why I crossed the street and gave me a ticket. A White lady crossed with me. I asked him why he gave me a ticket and not her. He said, I got you instead of her.

Matt described an experience where he worked at a factory job and was discriminated against on the basis of his race to the point where he was terminated:

> I was driving a 1995 Chevy Blazer and working at a Kroger in Grosse Pointe. I was dropping off a co-worker. I went back to pick up a co-worker. We were going to go out and the police followed me for a long time. I pulled over and they went slow. They pulled me over. I said, "What am I being pulled over for?" The cop said he was just seeing what's going on. He gave me a ticket and said if I don't come to court, he would come up to my job and arrest me. I felt that I was followed and harassed because I was Black—it was racist. Another situation I had was while working at a factory. A White lady always had her phone out texting. So I took mine out and started texting. She didn't get into trouble but an HR person came up to me and said, "Give me your cell phone." I said, "I'm not giving you my cell phone." She got hers out. She said, "I'm going to take your cell phone and break it." She said. "Let's go to the office." I said "Come on." I walked in front of her and beat her to the office and opened the door for her and she fired me. I told my dad and he called her. I was on the three-way and he said that's not right. My dad threatened to take them to court but eventually just dropped it.

Cal addressed a situation where he was stopped and arrested for wearing a certain hat. "The gang squad picked me up at about age 17 years old for walking with a golf hat on and kept me for seven hours." He further indicated that in 1983 in Dothan, Alabama, he didn't move out of the way for certain White people who were walking on the same sidewalk but coming from a different direction:

> The police pulled up and appeared upset and said, "Hey, boy, you know when people are walking you move out of the way, do you understand?" I felt concerned, it really bothered me that they were that mean and hateful towards me.

S recalled an incident in the military where he felt misperceived and verbally prejudged to be doing something wrong and was accosted and detained:

> Two Military Police (MPs) thought I was talking about them when I was talking about my dude, so they came up on me saying, "Let me see your ID because we heard what you said." But I said, "I wasn't talking to you."

R indicated there were two occasions where his brother-in-law was accosted by the police but released without a ticket:

> My brother-in-law and I were out once and they targeted him. They were patting his pockets down and stuff. We didn't have nothing!

> And I remember another time in front of his house. He was out in his car . . . getting something out of his car, and the cops pulled up and shined the light on him and three or four of them were all over. So I came out of the house, too, you know they looked at me and told me to step back! Ended up he didn't have nothing. Nothing!

Dr. Demetrius E. Ford Ph. D. J.D., Psy.D.

Feeling racially profiled/criminally stereotyped by people in authority.

Participants discussed how it was not only the police who racially profiled them but people In authorIty from other various disciplines. People in authority are those trusted with administrative power to give orders or make decisions.

J addressed the experience of being mistreated in general on the basis of his race:

> All my life I've been in the places where they did not expect me to be. The neighborhoods, the jobs, the hotels, the wherever. And I've . . . racial profiling has been a constant in my life up until, well, today! It's always a factor. You never know where you're going to get hit with it, the lack of respect, the suspicion, the aloneness of being a so-called . . . I don't want to put names on myself but a so-called successful Black man in America.

R. indicated that he once worked for an organization that incorrectly labeled him as lazy:

In the corporate world, I requested a developmental assignment in a specific area of the company in which I worked. I got the assignment, and once there the people didn't give me anything to do. And so I went to the first level manager, they call them the unit manager, that was the person that was supervising me directly. And I said, "Well it's been a couple of weeks, and I haven't really had an assignment" and this, that, and the other thing. And what I took upon myself to do was I read the employee handbook, rules, you know, this, that, and the other thing. All the written down stuff. And there's always the rules and there's always the unspoken rules, you know? So I knew a bit about how the company worked.

So I made a request, I'd like to sit in on a case, because this was a labor relations area okay. I'd like to sit in, blah, blah, blah, blah. I started getting clerical stuff. Okay? So now, you know, I'm making in excess of fifty grand a year and they're throwing clerical stuff at me? I said okay. So what I did, I'd date and time stamp stuff. And I just started keeping a record. But in the meantime I read everything that I possibly could on labor relations and all of that. And I also started reading about company culture and this and that. I just started educating myself. I said these people are not going to make a fool out of me and I'm not going to act the damn fool.

Well, one day, I can't remember what it was they wanted me to. This woman came and wanted me to use a copier and copy this big, giant document. That was like, I'm not doing that. But you know. So I went to the . . . I ended up going to the director, a White guy. And I told him, you know, that this was an unsatisfactory assignment. So he goes back, talks to the area manager, and when he called me up for the meeting he goes "They're telling me that you're not cooperative." And they told me this. And they told me that. And I'm going what? Not cooperative? And later on I found out that not only had they said I was uncooperative, they said I was surly, lazy; you see where this is going?

I went to the vice president at that point, because the vice president and I had worked together on a task force, and she knew what I could do. She had a report I had written. They took that report and put that whole piece, with minor changes, into this document. I also had worked on some re-engineering things within the company and also had been responsible for some pretty weighty reports. And sometimes my sections were adopted without any changes. I told her what was up. Then I brought up my document. She said, "I don't want to see that," she said "I trust you." She said, "You just go and you be quiet and the less you say about this going forward the better." In seven days I was out of there. And the area manager ended up with a reprimand. That was on the quiet but she told me. She said, "We took care of it." And he was hot. He was *hot*.

J addressed an occasion, as a youth, where he felt labeled and made a poster child for the poor so that a White charity could promote their organization and receive greater funding:

> And the people at the Pacific Garden Mission wanted to use me as a fundraising tool. They had me write a letter to their vast constituency in an attempt to, you know, we need money to take care of families like J's. They took my picture and they had me in there and they used me to . . . I remember the thing said 56 million Negroes a year are going into poverty. What can we do to help Negroes like J and his family? Please send a donation.

J indicated in reference to being unjustly stopped at Meijer that he felt that the Meijer security was trying to make him out to be the suspect:

> You could tell he wanted me to be the guy.

Mental trauma

Participants discussed how psychologically distressing their experiences of being targeted and accosted by the police were on the basis of their race. Many reported feeling helpless, frustrated, and angry. Some reported having lasting negative feelings regarding the police and authority. All participants experienced long-term effects.

Mental trauma was assessed by collecting verbal and nonverbal data; therefore, a nonverbal description will be provided with each narrative to supplement relevant data associated with tone of voice and nonverbal communications.

J relayed an experience at a Meijer store where he was detained and falsely imprisoned after being mistaken for or considered a possible suspect by police. J's tone of voice was as if he were re-experiencing the Meijer's experience all over again. His eyes widened. His vocal tone was sharp. His muscles tightened:

They detained me in the parking lot while the other cop went in and checked the video footage of the store and all the rest of the stuff. And when they came out, when the other cop came to the door and said "It's not him," this cop who was confronting me was visibly disappointed. You could tell he wanted me to be the guy, because he didn't like what I was saying to him in the parking lot confrontational wise, calling him . . . not calling him names but calling him out, telling him he had no reason to be stopping me: "No I'm not going to let him see what was in my bag, no, it's Fourth Amendment rights. I don't have to show you a damn thing, why did you stop me? You must be racial profiling me, there's no other reason to stop me." And he's getting madder and madder and madder.

Deo told of how he and friends were accosted by police. Deo's nonverbal expressions were inconsistent with his story. After explaining that his friend was hit by the police officer, Deo's eyebrows rose and his demeanor became defensive and he smiled as if he was trying to hide a feeling of powerlessness. Deo explained that the experience left him not liking any police. Therefore, it is apparent that the experience had a traumatic effect on him emotionally.

> One time they pulled us over and they pulled all of us out of the car and put us in handcuffs without saying anything. And I asked them, why are you putting us in handcuffs? And instead of him explaining why he did it, he hit one of my guys. He hit him. You know, hard. And it was funny to me.

Cal did not go into detail but his facial expressions indicated that he was distressed by his experience with a police officer in Dothan, Alabama who told him to move aside when a White person walks down the street. Cal's voice sounded as if he was pleading me to change the circumstance of the negative experience he had. He indicated that because he has experienced discrimination all his life, he has learned to expect it. His expressions appeared as though he felt that the kind of trauma he has experienced was somehow normal. Cal said, I felt concerned. It really bothered me that they were that mean and hateful towards us.

Fear

Some participants indicated that they were horrified by the experience. They were terrorized and apprehensive about what was happening and what was going to happen while being accosted.

S described a terrifying experience with the police when he was 16 years old. The police aggressively accosted him and made him sit in their back seat while they ransacked his car. S's tone of voice reflected shock and powerlessness. He also appeared defensive and victimized. But his feelings of victimization were magnified by the fact that the perpetrator was a police officer. Lastly his nonverbal communications were suggesting, "Why, what did I do wrong?" It appears as if he felt there was no justice.

When I was sixteen-seventeen years old, I was riding with a friend, and we got pulled over by police at a McDonalds— Gratiot and Seven Mile. The police told us to get out. They searched us, didn't ask for any registration, nothing. They tore up the car looking for guns, saying we fit the description of two Black men. No other justification for why they pulled us over or anything. They put us in the back of the squad car while they searched. When they didn't find anything, then they told us we could get out and we were free to go.

V expressed fear of driving in White communities because of

apprehension of being harassed and accosted by White police officers. While V was speaking in the third person, he was really talking about himself. His vocal tone and nonverbal communication suggested that he in fact is afraid to drive on the north side of Eight Mile Road in the Metro Detroit area. On the north side of Eight Mile Road is the suburb of Warren. Warren Police have a reputation for harassment and intimidation of Blacks.

> Well, I know it's kind of tough sometimes when you're driving. The police will harass you, especially if you go across Eight Mile. Most people don't want to go across Eight Mile. Because you'd be driving in a Black situation — you know, it's kind of tough.
>
> They kind of pick you out. As soon as they see you or pull up behind you, you know, just flick you for some odd reason they choose to.

Dan had an experience in which the police pulled guns on him and his friends for allegedly switching lanes without signaling. He indicated that this experience was intense and contributed to him no longer feeling free in America. Dan's nonverbal demeanor communicated that after the police pulled a gun on him he no longer felt free. The incident was so traumatic that it caused him to almost feel like a slave in a free country. Slavery was a time of terror for Blacks in America and for Dan to equate his experience with the police to slavery says a lot about how traumatic it was. Dan spoke in the present tense rather than in the past tense. He indicated that he no longer feels free, since this experience. Trauma seems to have had a lasting effect on him.

It was profound, you know, it just showed me, like the things I was taught at school wasn't the truth. I mean like, the whole thing that we were each equal. All this like we free and everybody supposed to treat everyone a type away. It's just that racism was real, that it exists. People just did it covertly, people did it another way. It brought light to different things I have learned and different things I thought up until that point. It really showed me that that the thing exists. It wasn't something that you just read about or heard about.

Distrust

Many participants no longer see the police as peace officers but as antagonists. Because many participants were attacked by the police when they should have been rescued, they are now suspicious of the police. These participants are doubtful that the police have their best interests at heart.

S had many negative encounters with the police and expressed his feelings regarding trusting them. S gave a synopsis statement explaining that his distrust for the police is based on historical patterns of being stopped unjustly. S is left with a conclusion about all police based on his experience with a few. S seems to be suggesting that he has been so traumatized by the police that he will not even consider the fact that there may be a rational basis for any future stops. Trauma can sometimes be measured by the future psychological effects it has on the victim.

I learned early police is not for us, and they are not our friends. So police need to understand: When they pull us over, we are not already in a comfortable position. So they shouldn't come with the whole innocent until proven guilty, we all know it's bullshit—it should be you're guilty until proven innocent. Stop telling us it's one thing and making it another.

Deo indicated that after a family member had an unjust, negative experience with the criminal justice system he now felt substantial distrust of the criminal justice system. Deo nonverbally seems to be connecting the police to the criminal justice system and expressing an aversion to both. His trauma is so pervasive that it is expanding its entities of distrust. This seems to suggest a deeper level of trauma that may not be readily removed but may take long-term interventions including community support and social and cultural empowerment.

My cousin, I ain't going to say no names, he's doing like 14 years or something. But it's something they don't know if he did it or not. They didn't never really give him really a chance to speak. They let one of the persons go scot-free. But they just gave [my cousin] all the years. And supposedly, my cousin didn't do it. The other guy that they let go did it. And they took [my cousin]. And my cousin, he didn't say a word. He didn't say like anything. It made me really worried about the justice system. Like why is it like that? Because the guy they let go had a paid lawyer. My cousin didn't.

R described an experience that he had with the police that caused him to think differently about the police and to lose respect and to be suspicious of them.

> Another time I got stopped and they started questioning me about something that had happened, and I didn't know anything about this! And they were kind of nasty. And I said, "Well," I said, "Well, I really don't know what you're talking about. My sister lives in the neighborhood," this, that, and the other thing. Do you know what the cat had the nerve to do? Ask me if I wanted to buy tickets to the policemen's field day when they figured out that they didn't have nothing. I'm like, yeah right. And fortunately I didn't have the money. If I had two dollars in my wallet it wasn't going to happen anyway. And even if I had some money I wouldn't have bought them from them. They really gave me a hard time.

R's voice expressed disbelief and frustration that the police would victimize him then turn around and asked him to buy a ticket. The look on R's face was one of paradoxical disbelief and rage. It reminded me of a Mike Tyson fight where Mike Tyson would knock out his opponent then go over to kiss him and apologize.

Anger

Many of the participants said that they experienced strong negative emotions associated with perceived mistreatment from the police. They felt terrorized and unjustly accosted and harassed by them.

J indicated that the anger he feels is a constant, resulting from ongoing criminal profiling and racial discrimination. But unlike many, he is a professional and has learned how to channel this frustration and anger in productive ways. He's learned ways to break the bonds of oppression.

> I've tasted much success in my life because I've always been the guy designed to do it. The rage, the anger, has fueled my desire to do so. Early on, it was to show them what a lie they were, but then ultimately it became my habit. And as you know, success is probably, probably the greatest drug. I don't care how strung out you get on crack or sex or any of them, when you get strung out on success you want it again.

Deo indicated that after he and friends were subjected to being unjustly accosted by the police, they had negative emotions and felt powerless.

> We got animosity against them because they just come. Like we all just got like narcotics on us and nobody had nothing.

Dev was extremely angry when the police officer would not help him. He had called the police because his roommate's friend was being hostile and refused to leave.

> So my question was to the police—this is what I was telling the police officer—being that you are here right now and nobody

> can go to jail over this person putting their hands on me, then if there's a body out here at my residence, are you also telling me that, because everybody will have different stories, that nobody is going to go to jail? Now, they never took this person to jail for real, they told me I needed to go downtown—talk to a detective so they can investigate the case, etc. Now, although that may be protocol, which, you know, is what had been told to me, I look at that as an injustice where the simple fact that if we are actually trying to stop violence or prevent violence that they did not actually do anything to stop it, but they let it escalate. To me that would be an injustice for any color.

In R's experience, the police unjustly stopped him, claiming they believed his car was stolen, and then they searched his vehicle without his consent. R, who is very small in stature, felt violated, angry, and helpless.

> One guy [a policeman] declared that my car was stolen. I'm like, so they're going all through my car, looking through this and that. Open the trunk, you know, in and out, just looking for stuff. I didn't have anything. And I remember I was really irked but it was like, I'm all of five eight, 135 pounds, there wasn't too much I could do other than just deal with it. And they moved me on.

Dev explained experiencing extreme anger towards the police for not aiding him after he was assaulted in his own home. The police failed to arrest or ask the perpetrator to leave. Dev described his anger:

I was actually bleeding when I was talking to police. It's not that I needed stitches, but my entire point . . . I was actually trying to prevented from the jump, when I told the police I didn't want this person over there.

S reported being angry about false charges of starting a riot and not complying with military police. He explained that the charges were trumped up and eventually dropped. However, the charges caused him to lose the opportunity to continue boxing in the military.

C was a passenger in a car with a few of his friends and was unlawfully pulled over. C indicated that he believes they were pulled over because of racial profiling and couldn't believe it. His friend the driver was extremely agitated.

> The driver was pretty irate about being stopped, didn't appreciate it. The police officer tried to get him to calm down. Told him after running his license plate, his license, that somebody had used his name and he let us all [unintelligible].

BV experienced much anger over being accused by a police officer of selling drugs in an apartment he lived in, but what made him most angry was when the officer physically assaulted him.

> The black police officer pushed my head in front of the vending machine. I went to the hospital. I tried to get a lawsuit but I couldn't go through with it because they said there were too many drugs being issued at that building.

Poverty

All participants with the exception of two were either poor as children or were raised in working poor families. Based on income earned most participants are still poor. They have low wage jobs, are living paycheck to paycheck, and are struggling to obtain the very basic necessities of life.

V described a life of growing up in poverty. He grew up in a single mother home with two sisters in Detroit. He also is still on a limited income that he stretches from month to month.

> My mom was a hard working mom and single. My dad wasn't

there but my mother raised me and two sisters.

Matt grew up in a working class poor family. While employed, Matt is working part-time but his household income places him under the poverty level.

Dan grew up in poverty with a single, working mother. He described his childhood experience as follows:

> It was rough for me specifically because we really didn't have that much. My mother, you know, she kind of did her best, working as many jobs that she could, not able to give me the best things but [I] was always seeing different things on TV and you know kids at school who had the better clothes and shoes. The only time I got clothes and shoes was around income-tax time or birthdays. So you know growing up it was rough. The main thing I was always taught was to keep my head up.

BV indicated that when he was growing up his family was extremely poor. He was raised by both parents but the family was still poor. He indicated that only his father worked but that his father would not buy him anything. Today BV supports himself on Social Security disability assistance.

> I had to drop out of high school at 16 to get a job at a liquor store so I could support my habits and get some money. My father wouldn't give me any money. And I worked there from when I was 16 to about 25.

Deo recalled growing up in poverty. His mother was on food stamps and always tried to make ends meet. There were times when Deo had to stay in a shelter for brief periods. He resided with other relatives. He moved from home to home and place to place. He focuses mostly on his adult life because he desires to forget much of the past. While he maintains full time work with two jobs, he still struggles to make ends meet. He often has to sacrifice certain things in order to pay his rent and utilities.

Prior to the age of four, Dev indicated that his parents were drug users and he grew up in poverty. Ark's mother was a teacher and he did not grow up in poverty. However, due to a lack of a positive father role model, he was influenced by negative peer groups. Consequently, he was incarcerated. Several felonies contribute to his low income, which is beneath the poverty level.

Feeling the American dream is a lie

Many participants seemed disappointed that they have not been able to move up the economic ladder of success. Instead, participants are entangled with feeling rejected and demonized by society as being criminals. Most participants have given up on prosperity and status in society and have created their own idea of success.

R indicated that he has struggled all his life to achieve the American dream, but he's now 63 years old and still has not received it. He's starting to see the light at the end of the tunnel but wishes the journey had not been so difficult and that that he could have achieved success at a much younger age. R now has a doctorate degree but still his wages are comparable to a White man with an Associate's or Bachelor's degree.

Ark indicated that he was railroaded and received an unjust sentence. He said that while in prison he was railroaded again and received an extended sentence. Because of his felony record, he finds it difficult to move ahead in life.

Deo indicated that poverty caused his mother to be distressed; consequently, he did not receive the support and guidance necessary to avoid the traps of society. But to be unjustly targeted by the police made matters worse; the felonies, convictions, and tickets locked him into a life of poverty and worry about the future.

S indicated that while incarcerated he was called a porch nigger and responded by calling the White person a KKK member. S seems not only to have given up on the American dream, but he sees that American dream as a false positive. He compares policemen to drug dealers and says that he doesn't need a gun to feel powerful.

Ark tells of a traumatic experience in prison where he lost faith in the American dream. He claims that he has had to reeducate himself and is now on a different path. He lives on a low income and has seen many opportunities and aspirations lost.

BV indicated that poverty in his family resulted in a hardened father who was unsupportive. Consequently he had to work and neglected his education. Due to the disconnect between him and his father, he was fathered and influenced by negative peers in the streets, which resulted in risk taking, selling drugs, and ultimately incarceration. In addition, he developed mental health problems and his American dreams vanished. He now has redefined success, which includes living in poverty and receiving SSI. On the other hand he has found strength in church and is often optimistic.

Re-storied Composite Narrative

The following is an amalgamated narrative based on the shared experiences of the participants. It summarizes, in narrative form, the major themes described above. It is similar to the composite depiction used in heuristic research (Moustakas, 1990).

The effect of demonizing participants as criminal appeared to be unjustified and traumatic. Participants were followed, stopped, questioned, accosted, and seized, then freed without incident. Participants felt that they were victimized and suffered psychological distress as a result of the profiling. Participants felt prejudged and told who they were (i.e., criminals) based on preconceived, unfounded notions. They felt that they were stereotyped based on police biases and fears that criminals should look like Black males. Participants felt powerless and not a part of the discussion with regard to what it means to be Black men who are disproportionately represented in the criminal justice system.

These co-researchers believe that they are the others, the outer group who have been told since slavery where to go, what to do, and who they are. These co-researchers seemed excited to explain that their assertiveness is not aggressiveness and that their education should not be interpreted as arrogance. What could participants do when the police, the very ones sworn to protect them, stalk them? Being followed is psychologically traumatizing in itself. How can participants trust those who violate their safety and their right to be left alone? The right to ride their cars in joy, go shopping freely, and not have to watch out for the police for fear of being stopped for driving while Black.

All participants in this study have had negative, embarrassing, and shameful experiences with the police, having been unjustly stopped, accosted, and interrogated. The trauma done is immeasurable. No matter how much education or success, all participants have experienced and continue to experience being followed, stared at, and made to feel uncomfortable.

Moreover, the research participants' experience of trauma is seen clearly in the urgency of the tone in their voices and the looks on their faces as they speak of it. Participants were reluctant to appear weak, as Black men, but there was a sense of powerlessness in their stories. Frustrated, angry, disempowered, they were crying out for help and attention. There was a paradox of feeling threatened by persons whom they could not stop and were not able to defend themselves against even though these same persons also represented access to justice and the rule of law. What seemed more dreadful for these participants was the fact that they did not know when or where the profiling would happen. Participants feared that profiling could occur at any time and could result in loss of their liberties through unjust incarceration or even threat or loss of their lives, as was seen in the cases of Malice Green, Trayvon Martin, Rodney King, Emmitt Till, Jonathan Ferrell, and others. This racial profiling trauma is like terrorism. J stated, "I got accosted by a policeman in Milwaukee because he didn't like my girlfriend's ethnicity. So he began to shout ethnic slurs and I began to shout curse words, and I got arrested and I spent the night or the weekend in jail. It was the N word."

After being stopped and accosted, most co-researchers were released with no ticket or citation. The police often apologized, as if the apology would cure the damage caused by the racial profiling. Co-researchers were relieved when they were not arrested or subjected to chains but were still left traumatized by the racial profiling experience. Are the illegal and unjust stops of co-researchers trending and pervasive in the American culture? This practice of racial profiling has not benefitted the co-researchers but has instead created traumas. The full extent of these psychological traumas was difficult to glean from participants, due to the shame associated with being profiled and treated so inhumanely.

Summary

In this chapter, I have presented the findings of my research. I have incorporated both narrative analysis and an analysis of the narrative in my approach to the data and presented a re-storied composite and an interpretive narrative. In the next chapter, I will provide a synopsis of the study, including a discussion of its limitations, implications for further research, and the personal meaning of this research, along with its social and psychological relevance.

Chapter V

Guns Down: Conclusions

This chapter provides a summary of each of the prior chapters and a review of the research findings. It also summarizes results and compares them with the literature review. Next it provides a discussion of the implications of this study and addresses limitations. It also gives recommendations for future research. The final portion of this chapter will discuss my personal reflections and describe my creative synthesis.

Dr. Demetrius E. Ford Ph. D. J.D., Psy.D.

Summary of Previous Chapters

The purpose of this study is to illuminate the experience of racial profiling through the narratives of 12 participants. Chapter I discussed the research question that inspired this process of inquiry: "What is the experience of Black men relative to criminal stereotypes?" I briefly described experiences from my own past that led to my current passion for this topic. I also discussed the social and clinical relevance of this research, as well as defined key terms.

Chapter II presented the findings of a thorough literature review; relevant literature was fashioned into themes of related material. The literature themes included racial profiling, trauma, anger, and poverty, and how they negatively affect Black men in America. A need for the current study was advocated based upon deficient research and literature on the psychological implications of racial profiling and the lack of research questioning the criminalblackman myth.

Chapter III discussed the qualitative methods of research employed, including the narrative model, and why these methods were selected for the current study. Furthermore, a brief history of the philosophy behind qualitative analysis, as well as a discussion of qualitative analysis itself, was offered. Finally, the specific methods and procedures used to gather and analyze the data were detailed. This process included the preparation and collection stages through storing, organizing, and analyzing the material. Finally, confidentiality and ethical standards were also discussed.

Chapter IV included the research findings and participant introductions. The research findings were presented using narrative methodology. The four themes that emerged were: racial profiling, mental trauma, anger, and poverty. Subthemes were fear and distrust.

Comparison of Research Findings to Literature Review

All of the themes in this research study were found in the literature. Of note is that all themes in the literature were not directly addressed in the study, as the research literature is broader. However, all the information discovered in literature is congruent with the findings in this study. The literature helped provide a foundation and a basis for understanding the research findings.

Racial profiling and feeling criminally stereotyped by people in authority

There are multiple types of racial profiling in literature. However, as it relates to Black men, most racial profiling involves perceptions that they are criminals. The criminal profiling process that increases the pool of Blacks incarcerated was seen in the crack/cocaine phenomenon that started in 1986 and ended when President Obama signed the Fair Sentencing Act in 2010. Blacks were penalized 100 times more than Whites who used powder cocaine, even though powder cocaine is chemically identical. Research by Reinarman and colleagues (1997) showed that crack users were no more violent than powder cocaine users.

The literature also identifies how thousands of Blacks and Hispanics have been unjustly racially profiled. An example of this was seen in the New York Police stop, question, and frisk policy (Bruinis, 2013). Over 2.8 million stops were made from 2004 to 2009. Over 50 percent of the stops were Blacks and 30 percent were Latino. Only 10 percent involved Whites even though the majority of New York residents are White. The U.S. Federal District Court for the Southern District of New York struck down the policy, calling it city-sanctioned racial profiling (Harvard Law Review, 2013). Becker (1963) indicated that the American criminal justice system targets minorities who are more likely to be accosted and prosecuted.

All participants in this study gave multiple detailed accounts of being racially profiled. They were followed, misidentified, threatened, stopped for what is called driving while Black, and in most cases, not ticketed. The participants' stories were consistent with research about racial profiling. Katheryn Russell-Brown (1998) used the stereotypic myth criminalblackman to describe how people associate young Black men with crime in America. The unjustified stops, questioning, and frisks in New York, as well as those reported in this study support findings in the literature review. Moreover, participants' stories of being stereotyped and profiled are congruent with results from the study on the Ionia Prison inmates in which Black men were misdiagnosed with schizophrenia after protesting poor conditions (Metzl, 2010).

Mental trauma

A study by Dressler, Oths, and Gravlee (2005) indicated that being a victim of racist stereotypes results in stress that contributes to health and disease. Moreover, Fang and Myers (2004) examined the negative consequences that discrimination has on health, quality of life, and life span. They discovered that Black men who were discriminated against and who consequently held in frustrations had higher blood pressure. High blood pressure is one of the leading causes of death for Black men.

Participants discussed the psychological distress of their experiences of being targeted and accosted by the police on the basis of race. This information is congruent with the literature review on health and racism. J indicated that he was traumatized for being falsely imprisoned at a Meijer store where the police were looking for a Black male suspected of stealing. Deo indicated that after he and a few friends were pulled over for a traffic violation, police officers put them all in handcuffs and hit one with his hand. It should be noted that Black men are not the most forward people when it comes to disclosing mental distress or assaults upon them. Through listening to their stories and observing their expressions, however, it became clear that mental distress and trauma was present.

Fear

Fear is something that most Black men from my experience are not willing to admit. Participants' stories all reflected their fears of the accosting authority. It appears that a significant cause of the fear was because the police usually carry weapons. The fear seems associated with these encounters because they were shocking. S described a terrifying experience with the police when he was 16 years old. The police aggressively accosted him and made him sit in their back seat while they ransacked his car. The fear associated with these experiences was the fear of feeling powerless and not knowing whether participants were going to be arrested and separated from their loved ones.

The literature suggests that the fear that Black men have relative to White men with guns is rooted in forced migration of their ancestors from Africa to be slaves (Palmer, 2002). Throughout slavery, Reconstruction, and Jim Crow, Black men were oppressed by White police officers and presumed guilty and often deprived of their constitutional rights. Even during the civil rights era when Blacks tried to stand up for their rights they were mistreated and beaten by the Police (Goluboff, 2007). Blacks suffered police brutality and were lynched often with the assistance and/or silence of the police.

A recent example referenced in the literature is the fear that Trayvon Martin experienced when he was accosted by George Zimmerman. His fear led to his preemptive self-defense (Farhi, 2012). It was unfortunate that an all-White jury with one White Hispanic could not get beyond a Black man who was being hunted like an animal acting in self-defense.

Likewise, the participants' experiences of fear connected with trauma resulting from being racially profiled are similar to the construct of fear seen in the literature review. The difference is that today Black men have more legal remedies, whereas in the past, Black men had little or no support from the police or the justice system. Another similarity is that fear has not lessened since racial profiling by the police continues, as evidenced by the New York stop, question, and frisk crisis (Bruinis, 2013).

Distrust

The distrust that participants were left with seemed to be long lasting. This distrust is connected to the fear generated by their traumatic experiences. All participants with the exception of one indicated that they still do not trust the police. They told of how they feel apprehension regarding police officers because of their negative experiences with them. They indicated that they try to avoid the police.

This distrust is seen in the literature in the fractured and suspicious relationship that Blacks have had with those entrusted with authority dating back to the times of slavery. Cartwright (1851) used the Bible to justify slavery, quoting it to say that slaves are to be obedient to their masters; whipping was Cartwright's cure for Drapetomania. That laws existed at that time to justify slavery legally and morally furthered the distrust that Blacks had for those entrusted with authority. A hundred and fifty years later, those entrusted with authority to keep the peace are still racially profiling Black men as criminals. Therefore, the research and the literature are congruent on the distrust issues that Black men have with regard to the police.

The distrust that Blacks have for the police is rooted in the Antebellum South and has continued through the Reconstruction and the civil rights era to the present. Throughout, Blacks have experienced a disproportionate incarceration rate compared to Whites relative to the percentage of Blacks in the United Sates. Matt, who desires to become a police officer, indicated that he does not trust police officers because they used to follow and harass him. One officer, after following and giving him a ticket, told Matt that if he did not show up for court he would come to his job and arrest him. Matt indicated that he wants to become a police officer to change the way officers treat citizens. This does not mean that Matt has no trauma or distrust relative to police officers, but it may suggest that he is further along in his healing from the trauma than the other participants in this study. The word mistrust also means misgivings and anxiety. This connection between Black men and anxiety surrounding the police is a common theme in the academic literature. Some of this traumatic distrust seems to be vicarious. Deo indicated that in court he saw his cousin receive a large sentence and the actual perpetrator go free. He indicated that this left a lasting scar on him relative to trusting the police and the court system.

Anger

The existing body of literature shows that many Black men have strong aversive emotions towards the police and those in authority who Black men perceive have abused their positions. This was certainly seen in the Trayvon Martin case, where Trayvon was angry that he was racially profiled by George Zimmerman and this led to his preemptive self-defense (Farhi, 2012). Martin Luther King Jr., a peaceful person, railed against racial injustices and marched for justice. Slaves angered by slavery rebelled against their masters and oppression and fought for the Union army in the Civil War (Painter, 2010).

The anger seen in Black men, according to the literature, is the product of mistreatment resulting from being Black. In this study, Black men expressed anger due to being penalized falsely. Some were incarcerated and some received longer sentences than they should have. All were unjustly stopped and interrogated, some were frisked and assaulted, and no apologies were ever given by the police. As a result of feeling violated and having no recourse for justice, they became angered.

Moreover, several participants felt anger because they felt that the police had preconceived, negative ideas about them before they were stopped. This pattern is congruent with stereotypes and labels directed towards Blacks in the literature. Research by Katz and Braly (1933) found that the traits attributed mostly to Negroes were superstitious, lazy, happy-go-lucky, ignorant, musical, ostentatious, very religious, stupid, physically dirty, naive, slovenly, and unreliable.

Poverty and feeling the American dream is a lie

Poverty has been a common theme in the history of Black men. Dating back to slavery, Black men built the wealth of their masters and this nation as their masters paid taxes on their wealth. But Black men were never paid. Even in share cropping, Blacks were cheated. In prison leasing, Black men often are not paid. Jim Crow laws in the South have kept Blacks away from fair employment remuneration. Today Black men are not paid equitably to White men for the same performance and education levels

The literature suggests that poverty historically has been a reality for Blacks. In 2007, 34% of Black children under age 18 lived in poverty, compared with 10% of White children, and 27% of Hispanic children (U.S. Census Bureau, 2008). This existing literature is consistent with participants' stories of being raised in poverty. Moreover, most of the men interviewed still remained in poverty. J indicated that about a year ago he struggled with poverty even though he was very successful at one point in his adult life. Eight out of 12 participants still face poverty as the working poor or were seeking employment. One of the participants receives social security disability. Therefore, participants still face poverty today.

Is poverty directly connected with crime or being Black? What is the link between poverty, crime, and Black men? Consider the following: crime is associated with being poor. The literature review supports that Black men are discriminated in employment and historically have faced poverty. Therefore the logical syllogism is to conclude that Black men are criminals. The problem with this is that what is logical is not always true. In order to have a true conclusion, one must also have a true premise. The first premise regarding poverty and crime is false. There are criminals at all income levels and the myth that the King can do no wrong has long been dispelled.

How this Study Adds to the Current Body of Literature

There has been much research on Black men and crime but most of it seems to be quantitative and not written from the perspective of Black men themselves. Most research on Black men has been written by people who use statistics to prove that since Black men are found at higher rates in the criminal justice system then they must be more criminal. This present study does not dispute the quantitative statistics but gives an alternative explanation of why Black men are disproportionately incarcerated. This study also questions traditional definitions of crime that are reluctant to call out White collar crime and fail to consider the selective prosecution of Black males and the disproportionate and excessive sentencing they experience. This question sees racial profiling as a crime itself and the victims of this crime being Black men.

This study also adds to the body of research in psychology by addressing the phenomenon of racial profiling, which influences the identity formation of Black men. It addresses the trauma that Black men experience as a result of racial profiling. This construct seems congruent with the new category in the DSM5 on trauma and other stress disorders (DSM 5, 2013).

This research contributes to criminology by providing another perspective on crime and Black men. It also contributes to an understanding of prevailing law and the Constitution. The Fourth Amendment addresses unreasonable searches and seizures. This study advocates interpreting the Fourth Amendment to protect the rights of all citizens, including Black males, and provides a theoretical basis for the claims of victims of the New York Police Department's stop, question, and frisk policy.

This research also contributes to issues of civil rights and other issues at the intersection of race and society by raising awareness of the practice of racial profiling. African American Studies departments and multicultural curriculums will be affected by this research as it corroborates current theories related to race and society. Most research fails to take into consideration the effects of trauma resulting from racial profiling. Other interesting issues that have been raised in this study are distrust in systems, depression, and lack of belief in and motivation for pursuing the American dream.

Implications and Potential Applications

By illuminating the experience of Black men relative to criminal stereotypes, I hope to increase the awareness of this marginalized and misunderstood population. I aspire to increase research in the area of eradicating racial profiling relative to Black men being criminals. As a result, Black men will be able to feel truly free in a society where they don't have to worry about being accosted, traumatized, and criminalized, but will be able to enjoy the pursuit of life, liberty, and happiness. What is at stake is not just the liberation of the Black man but the healing of our society by improving race relations and removing the epidemic of racial profiling.

This multidisciplinary topic is relevant and has implications across disciplines. Racial profiling affects the way police do policing. It counters civil rights as seen in the Trayvon Martin case. It goes against Constitutional Law in that the Fourth Amendment protects citizens from unreasonable searches and seizures. It has an impact on psychology, psychiatry, and counseling in addressing trauma Black men experience as a result of being racially profiled.

The Obama Administration in 2014, broadened federal protections under the racial profiling, law-enforcement reporting policy. This study is on the cutting edge because it addresses the contemporary issue of racial profiling; therefore, this study can be a model of methodological approaches to understanding the implications of racial profiling and providing a remedy. This study can also serve to provide insight on the racial profiling of Hispanics relative to illegal immigration stereotypes and Arabs relative to terrorism stereotypes.

Limitations of This Study

While the goal of this study was not to find generalizable facts, it is still important to explicitly state that there are some limitations regarding to what, in quantitative research, is referred to as external and internal validity. As there was not a statistically adequate pool of participants, the themes are not generalizable to all Black men. This lack of external validity is a common feature of qualitative research.

Connected to this external limitation, internal validity is also a common criticism of qualitative research. That is, how does the researcher insure that he or she is accurately describing the data? Here it is important to remember that the truths sought by narrative researchers are "narrative truths not historical truths" (Polkinghorne, 2007, p. 479). That is, although the data being researched—the narratives of black men regarding criminal stereotypes—have not been quantitatively measured, in collecting and recoding the stories I made every effort to truthfully record the actual and intended meaning of the participants. After the data was analyzed, themes discovered, and narrative summaries compiled, participants were given the opportunity to review and correct their statements. All reported that the narrative descriptions were accurate representations of what they had each intended to express. This "trustworthiness" is essential to the qualitative method.

Assessing trauma may have been another weakness of this study. It appears to me that Black men may have a difficult time disclosing victimization issues; however, I used my clinical skills and active listening to try to understand the substantive nature of the trauma experienced. While I was able to glean much information, it appeared there was more left to discover. Therefore, in addition to data gathering through narrative storytelling, it may be helpful for future studies to integrate an objective test for assessing trauma.

While I suspect that Black senior citizens would have had similar, racial profiling experiences, another limitation was that my oldest participant was only 61 years old.

Recommendations for Future Research

Future research should include police officers' experiences regarding stopping, questioning, and arresting Black men. What is the experience of a police officer when questioning a Black suspect? Discussing the relationship between police officers and the Black citizens they have sworn to protect would add depth to the social narrative.

In addition, there were no White male participants in this study because the specific investigation concerned the experience of Black men. While White men do not experience racially motivated police harassment such as "stop & frisk" or "driving while Black" that Black citizens, and in particular Black men, experience, the White experience of being questioned by police would be an interesting juxtaposition to the narratives presently being discussed. Comparing and contrasting both the immediate experience and the long term consequences of each racial/ethnic perspective would further detail the differences that Black men experience in relation to the law.

I hope this study motivates others to further research how criminal stereotypes affect the identity formation, as well as the health, safety, and welfare, of Black men. The findings presented here contribute to the foundation of literature on trauma resulting from racial profiling. They also suggest that quantitatively exploring trauma would be helpful. Towards that goal, the development of an assessment protocol to measure trauma in Black men resulting from racial profiling is suggested. This, along with narrative data, would help us better understand the consequences of criminal stereotypes that Black men have to contend with on a regular basis.

Personal Reflections and Creative Synthesis

The right to not be searched and seized without probable cause is fundamental to the Bill of Rights and the U.S. Constitution. The right to not be negatively discriminated against on the basis of one's race is protected by the 14th Amendment of the U.S. Constitution. Higgins, Jennings, Jordan, and Gabbidon (2011) studied the relationship between race and decisions by police officers to search. Results indicated that Blacks were searched significantly more than Whites and Hispanics. Higgins and colleagues (2011) concluded that race not ethnicity was the causative factor in decisions to search.

Racial profiling violates these rights simultaneously. This stereotyping of Black men results in psychological trauma. What compounds this problem is that the trauma never heals because the existence of racial profiling is disputed in America. My concern is that racial profiling is pervasive but often implicit. This crime perpetrated on Black men must be addressed in order for this epidemic to end.

It is time to see racial profiling for what is: An epidemic. It not only targets Black men who may not wear the socially appropriate attire, but it confronts all Black men whether they are aware of it or not. Retired Federal Appeals Court Judge Damon Keith, who is 91 years old, once told me the story of being racially profiled after co-presiding over the 1976 Bicentennial Conference of Federal Judges, organized around the 200-year anniversary of the signing of the Declaration of Independence. After the conference ended and he was on his way out, a White gentleman, thinking he was a valet, kindly asked Judge Keith if he would get his car for him. This, of course, is not unfamiliar to Black citizens, regardless of their education, social position or actual job.

I have been privileged and honored to participate in this narrative study that has explored and challenged traditional notions of African American men, which mostly describe them quantitatively, without their input, as criminals. This task has been a labor of love. Reviewing literature and relevant research, writing and rewriting, analyzing and reanalyzing data have led me to conclude that the voices of the participants in this study will provide insight into the phenomenon of the Black male as criminal stereotype. Moreover, this study gives insight into what can be done to change things so that Black men will not continue to have negative experiences of being stereotyped as criminals.

In retelling the participants' stories, I have gained greater insight into and understanding of mental health through the eyes of the participants, as opposed through the mind of the analyst or statistics only. I believe that this exploration has given me a huge impetus to advocate for justice and empowerment of the oppressed. I have a renewed commitment to scholarship and leadership to promote justice for all. Psychological health is directly connected with existential perceptions of freedom and a pathway to life, liberty, and the pursuit of happiness. Finally, I'd like to thank all the participants because without them this narrative inquiry would not have been possible.

Summary

In this final chapter, I have presented and compared the findings of this study with the existing literature. I have explored the social and psychological implications of the study, as well as considered its validity, limitations, and implications for future research. In conclusion, I have discussed personal reflections and the meaning of the study. Using the narrative methodology, I set out to discover the experience of Black men relative to being stereotyped as criminals. I have done this by entering into the lived experiences of my study participants, representing and interpreting their stories, while respecting them as the experts of their own lives.

This unique experience gathered the voices of Black men and, the research confirmed that Black men have been subjected to the trauma of being victimized through the crime of racial profiling. Racial profiling subjects Black men to disproportionate criminal charges, prosecutions, convictions, sentencing, and disenfranchisement when attempting to reenter and reintegrate into the community. Black men convicted of felonies have an extremely difficult time locating employment. Finally, between 10 and 13% of Black men are not allowed to vote, due to felony disenfranchisement laws (Bowers & Preuhs, 2009). As a narrative researcher, I hope this work will contribute to the research community and society at large and will provoke the emergence of more hopeful, life-enhancing stories of Black men.

References

A

Adams, M. S., Robertson, C. T., Gray-Ray, P., & Ray, M. C. (2003). Labeling and delinquency. Adolescence, 38, 171-186.

Adorno, T. W., Frenkel-Brunswik, E., Levinson, D. J., & Sanford, R. N. (1950). The authoritarian personality. New York, NY: Norton.

Allport, G. (1979). The nature of prejudice. Cambridge, MA: Perseus Books.

Altman, N. (2010). The analyst in the inner city: Race, class and culture through a psychoanalytic lens. New York, NY: Taylor & Francis.

Alvesson, M. (2007). Reflexivity. In G. Ritzer (Ed.), Blackwell Encyclopedia of Sociology. Retrieved from http://www.blackwellreference.com/public/book?id=g9781405124331_9781405124331

American Pscyhiatric Association (2013). Diagnostic & Statistical Manual of Mental Disorders 5th Edition. Arlington, VA: American Psychiatric Association.

Anderson, T. H. (2003). The pursuit of fairness: A history of affirmative action. New York, NY: Oxford University Press.

Archer, J. (1994). Male Violence. New York, NY: Routledge.

Asante, K. (2002). 100 greatest African Americans: A biographical encyclopedia. Amherst, NY. Prometheus Books.

Basler, R. P. (1946). Abraham Lincoln: His selected speeches and writings. Cleveland, OH: World Publishing.

Becker, H. S. (1963). Outsiders: Studies in the sociology of deviance. New York, NY: The Free Press.

Behrendt, S. D., Richardson, D., & Eltis, D. (1999). Transatlantic Slave Trade. In A. Appiah & H. L. Gates (Eds.), Africana: The encyclopedia of the African and African American experience. New York, NY: Basic Civitas.

Bell, E. L., & Nkomo, S. (2001). Our separate ways: Black and White women and the struggle for professional identity. Boston, MA: Harvard Business School Press.

Berdahl, J. L., & Min, J. (2012). Prescriptive stereotypes and workplace consequences for East Asians in North America. Journal of Cultural Diversity and Ethnic Minority Psychology, 18, 141–152.

Bjorkqvist, K. (1994). Sex differences in physical, verbal and indirect aggression: A review of recent research. Sex Roles, 30, 177-188.

Blair, N. A. (2011), Illegal immigration overstays its welcome: How the criminalization of unlawful presence in America would help relieve inadequacies in Federal immigration law. Ave Maria Law Review 10(1), 203-223.

Bleakley, A. (2005). Stories as data, data as stories: Making sense of narrative inquiry in clinical education. Medical Education, 39, 540-554.

Bly, R. (1990). Iron John: A book about men. Cambridge, MA: Da Capo Pres

Bowers, M. M., & Preuhs, R. R. (2009). Collateral consequences of a collateral penalty: The negative effect of felon disenfranchisement laws on the political participation of nonfelons. Social Science Quarterly 90, 722–743.

Brown v. Board of Education of Topeka, 347 U.S. 483 (1954).

Bruinis, H. (2013). How to revamp NYPD's "Stop and Frisk" policy? That's the hard part. The Christian Science Monitor.

Bruner, J. (1990). Acts of meaning. Cambridge, MA: Harvard University Press.

Bull, P. (2001). State of the art: Nonverbal communication, The Psychologist, 14, 644-647.

Butler, S. (2009). Mamie Katherine Phipps Clark (1917-1983). Encyclopedia of Arkansas History & Culture (pp. 12-27). Little Rock, AR: CALS.

Cartwright, S. A. (1851) Diseases and Peculiarities of the Negro Race. Retrieved from http://www.pbs.org/wgbh/aia/part4/4h3106t.html

Christensen, R., Barlow, L., & Ford, D. E. (2013). A moment to come together: Personal reflections of Trayvon Martin. Journal of Social Action, Psychology and Counseling, 5, 131–137.

Christman, H. M. (1959). The Published papers of Chief Justice Earl Warren. New York, NY: Simon and Shuster.

Cinnerela, M. (1998). Manipulating stereotype rating tasks: Understanding questionnaire context effects on measures of attitudes, social identity and stereotypes. Journal of Community & Applied Social Psychology, 8, 345–362.

Cirillo, L., Kaplan, B., & Wapner, S. (1989). Emotions in ideal human development. Hillsdale, NJ: Lawrence Erlbaum Associates.

Clandinin, D. (2007). Handbook of narrative inquiry: Mapping a methodology. Thousand Oaks, CA: SAGE.

Clandinin, D. J., & Connelly, F. M. (2000). Narrative inquiry: Experience and story in qualitative research. San Francisco, CA: Wiley.

Clandinin, D., & Connelly, F. M. (2004). Narrative inquiry: Experience and story in qualitative research. San Fransisco, CA: Jossey-Bass.

Cohen, W. (1976). Negro involuntary servitude in the south, 1865 – 1940: A Preliminary Analysis. Journal of Southern History, 42, 31-60.

Cohen, J. W., & Harvey, P. J. (2006). Misconceptions of gender: Sex, masculinity, and the measurement of crime. The Journal of Men's Studies, 14, 223-233.

Cooley, C. H. (1922). Human nature and the social order. New York, NY: Charles Scribner's Sons.

Compton, R. E. (1993). Just the melanin in the skin: The experience of discrimination. Unpublished master's thesis, Center for Humanistic Studies, Detroit, MI.

Correll, J., Park, B., Judd, C. M., & Wittenbrink, B. (2007). The influence of stereotypes on the decision to shoot. European Journal of Social Psychology. 37, 1102–1117.

Corsini, R. J. (1999). The Psychology Dictionary. New York, NY: Routledge.
Cortazzi, M. (1993). Narrative analysis. London: Falmer Press.

Creswell, J. W. (2009). Research design: Qualitative, quantitative and mixed methods approaches. Thousand Oaks, CA: SAGE.

Crotty, M. (1998). The foundations of social science research: Meaning and perspective in the research process. Thousand Oaks, CA: SAGE.

Curry, G. E. (1996). The affirmative action debate. Reading, MA: Addison-Wesley Publishing Company, Inc.

Delgado, R., & Stefanic, J. (2000). Critical Race Theory: An introduction. New York, NY: NYU Press.

Derrida, J. (1981). Positions. Baltimore, MD: Johns Hopkins University Press. Dressler, W. W., Oths, K. S., & Gravlee, C. C. (2005). Race and ethnicity in public health research: Models to explain health disparities. Annual Review of Anthropology, 34, 231-252.

Du Bois, W. E. B. (1965). The souls of Black folk. New York, NY: Bantam Classic.

Dvorak, R. (1999). Cracking the code: decoding colorblind slurs during the congressional crack cocaine debates. Michigan Journal of Race and Law, 5, 611-652.

Eagly, A. H., & Beall, A. E. (2004). The psychology of gender. New York, NY: Guilford Press.

Eichrodt, W., & Smith, K. Man in the Old Testament. Chicago, IL: Henry Regnery Publishing Company.

Etherington, K. (2004). Becoming a reflective researcher. Philadelphia, PA: Kingsley.

Etherington, K. (2007). Ethical research in reflective relationships. Qualitative Inquiry, 13, 599-616. doi:10.1177800407301175

Fair Sentencing Act (2010). Public Law 111–220.

Fang, C. Y., & Myers, H. F. (2001). The effects of racial stressors and hostility on cardiovascular reactivity in African American and White men. Health Psychology, 20, 64–70. doi: 10.1037//0278-6133.20.1.64

Falk, B. & Blumenreich, M. (2005). The power of questions: A guide to research for teachers and students. Portsmouth, NH: Heinemann.

Farhi, P. (April 12, 2012). Trayvon Martin Story Found in the Media. Washington D.C: Washington Post.

Fisher v. University of Texas at Austin, 570 U.S. (2013).

Feagin, J. R., & McKinney, K. D. (2003). The many costs of racism. Lanham, MD: Rowman and Littlefield.

Fiske, S. T. (1993). Controlling other people: The impact of power on stereotyping. American Psychologist, 48, 621–628.

Freeman, J. B., Schiller, D., Rule, N. O., & Ambady, N. (2010). The neural origins of superficial and individuated judgments about in-group and out-group members. Human Brain Mapping, 31, 150–159.

G

Gabbidon, S. L, Greene, H. T, & Yong, V. D. (2002). African American classics in criminology and criminal justice. Thousand Oaks, CA: SAGE Publications.

Gaertner, S. L., & McLaughlin, J. P. (1983). Racial stereotypes: Associations and ascriptions of positive and negative characteristics. Social Psychology Quarterly, 46, 23–30.

Garner, B. A. (2009). Black's law dictionary (9th Ed.). St. Paul, MN: West Publishing.

Gates Jr., H. L. (2009). Was Lincoln a racist? Retrieved from http://www.theroot.com/articles/history/2009/02/was_lincoln_a_racist.html

Gilbert, G. M. (1951). Stereotype persistence and change among college students. Journal of Abnormal and Social Psychology, 46, 245–254.

Gold, M. E., & Richards, H. (2012). To label or not to label. The special education question for African Americans. Education Foundations 26 (1-2): 143–156.

Goldman, R., & Gallen, D. (1992). Thurgood Marshall: Justice for all. New York, NY: Carroll & Graf.

Goluboff, R. L. (2007). The lost promise of civil rights. Cambridge, MA: Harvard University Press.

Goodman M., Tagle, D., Fitch. D., Bailey, W., Czelusniak, J., Koop, B., Benson, P., & Slightom, J. (1990). Primate evolution at the DNA level and a classification of hominoids. Journal of Molecular Evolution, 30, 260–266. doi:10.1007/BF02099995

Grossman, L. K. (2001). From bad to worse: Black images on "White" news. Columbia Journalism Review, 40(2), 55.

Gutiérrez-Jones, C. (2001). Critical race narratives: A study of race, rhetoric, and injury. New York, NY: New York University Press.

Hagedorn, John M. (1998). Gang violence in the post industrial era. In M. Tonry and M. H. Moore (Eds.), Youth violence. Chicago, IL: University of Chicago Press.

Haig, D. (2004). The inexorable rise of gender and the decline of sex: Social change in academic titles, 1945–2001. Archives of Sexual Behavior, 33, 87–96.

Harper, F. D. (2005). Editor's Comments. Journal of Negro Education, 74, 19.

Harvard Law Review (2013). Civil Procedure. Class Actions, Southern District of New York Certifies class Action Against City Police for suspicionless stops and frisks of Blacks and Latinos 126(3).

Helms, J. E. (2007). Race is a nice thing to have: A guide to being a White person or understanding the White persons in your life (2nd Ed.). Alexandria, VA: Microtraining Associated, Inc.

Higgins, G. E., Jennings, W. G., Jordan, K. L., & Gabbidon, S. L. (2011). Racial profiling in decisions to search: A preliminary analysis using propensity-score matching. International Journal of Police Science & Management 13, 336-347.

Hill, C. E., Thompson, B. J., & Williams, E. N. (1997). A guide to conducting consensual qualitative research. The Counseling Psychologist, 25, 517–572.

Hooks, B. (2004). We real cool: Black men and masculinity. New York, NY: Routledge.

Izumi, Y., & Hammonds, F. (2007). Changing ethnic/racial stereotypes: The roles of individuals and groups. Social Behavior and Personality, 35, 845-852.

Jacobs, H. (2003). The incidents in the life of a slave girl. Mineola, NY: Dover Publishing Inc.

Jones, C., & Kaplan, M. F. (2003). The effects of racially stereotypical crimes on juror decision-making and information-processing strategies. Basic and Applied Social Psychology 25, 1–13.

Josselson, R., & Lieblich, A. (Eds.). (1999). Making meaning of narratives; the narrative study of lives. Thousand Oaks, CA: SAGE.

Judd, C. M., & Park, B. (1993). Definition and assessment of accuracy in social stereotypes. Psychological Review 100, 109–128.

Karlins, M., Kauffman, T., & Walters, G. (1969). On the fading of social stereotypes: Studies in three generations of college students. Journal of Personality and Social Psychology, 13, 1–16.

Katz, D., & Braly, K. (1933). Racial stereotypes of one hundred college students. Journal of Abnormal and Social Psychology, 28, 280–290.

Kelly, S. D., Barr, D. J., Church, R. B., & Lynch, K. (1999). Offering a hand to pragmatic understanding: The role of speech and gesture in comprehension and memory. Journal of Memory and Language, 40, 577-592.

Khenti, A. A. (2013). Homicide among young Black men in Toronto: An unrecognized public health crisis? Canadian Journal of Public Health 104, 12-14.

Kimmel, M. (1996). Manhood in America: A cultural history. New York. Free Press.

Knorr-Cetina, K. (1993) Strong Constructivism—from a sociologist's point of view: A personal addendum to Sismondo's paper. Social Studies of Science 23, 553-563.

Krienert, J. L. (2003). Masculinity and crime: A quantitative exploration of Messerschmidt's Hypothesis. Retrieved from http://sociology.org/content/vol7.2/01_krienert.html

Kunjufu, J. (1986). Countering the conspiracy to destroy Black boy II. Sauk Village, IL: African American Images.

L

Landsford, J. E. (2002) Boys' and girls' relational and physical aggression in nine countries. Aggressive Behavior, 38, 298–308.

Lemert. E. M. (1951). Social pathology: A systematic approach to the theory of sociopathic behavior. New York, NY: McGraw-Hill.

Lence, R. M. (1992). Union and liberty: The political philosophy of John C. Calhoun. Indianapolis, IN: Liberty Fund.

Leslie P. L. (1991). Black Southern professional women: Struggles and contributions (Doctoral dissertation, Boston University). Dissertation Abstracts International, 51(09). 3037A.

Levy, P. B. (1998). The civil rights movement. Westport, CT: Greenwood Press.

Link, B. G., Cullen, F. T., Struening, E. L., Shrout, P. E., & Dohrenwend, B. P. (1989). A modified labeling theory approach to mental disorders: An empirical assessment. American Sociological Review, 54, 400–423.

Lippman, W. (1922). Public opinion. Illinois: Watchmaker Publishing

Locke, L., Spirduso, W. W., & Silverman, S. (2000). Research proposals that work (4th Ed.). New York, NY: SAGE.

Longmore, P, (2013). Is inequality shortening your life span? White, black, or brown, we'd all live longer in a more equal, less status-driven society. The Washington Monthly, 45(1-2), 34.

Loevy, R. D. (1997), The Civil Rights Act of 1964: The passage of the law that ended racial segregation, Albany, NY: State University of New York Press.

MacMaster, K., Donovan, L., & MacIntyre, P. D. (2002). The effects of being diagnosed with a learning disability on children's self-esteem. Child study Journal, 3?, 101-108.

Mahar, W. (1998). Behind the burnt cork mask: Early blackface minstrelsy and Antebellum American popular culture. Chicago, IL: University of Illinois Press.

Manusov, V. (2005). The source of nonverbal measures: Going beyond words. Mahwah, NJ: Lawrence Erlbaum Associates.

Maple, M., & Edwards, H. (2010). Locating and understanding voices in narrative inquiry: A journey of discovery. In V. Minichiello & J. Kottler (Eds.) Qualitative journeys: Student and mentor experiences with research (pp. 33-48). Los Angeles, CA: SAGE.

Martinez, A. G., Piff, P. K., & Mendonza-Denton, R. (2011). The power of a label: Mental illness diagnoses, ascribed humanity and social rejection. Journal of Social and Clinical Psychology, 30, 1-23.

Marshall, C., & Rossman, G. (2006). Designing qualitative research. London, England: SAGE.

Martinez, E. (1993). Beyond Black/White: The racisms of our time. Social Justice, 20, 22–34.

Maslow, A. H. (1944). Deprivation, threat and frustration. Psychological Review, 48, 364-366.

Masur, L. P. (2011). The Civil War: A concise history. New York, NY: Oxford University Press.

Mead, H. M. (1914). The social self. The Journal of Philosophy, Psychology and Scientific Methods, 10(14), 374–380.

Mead, M. (1955). The expressions of emotions in man and animals by Charles Darwin. New York, NY: Philosophical Library.

Messerschmitt, J. W. (1993). Masculinities and crime: Critique and reconceptualization of theory. Lanham, MD: Rowan & Littlefield Publishers, Inc.

Messerschmitt, J. W. (1997). Crime as structured action: Gender, race, class and crime in the making. Thousand Oaks, CA: SAGE Publications.

Messerschmitt, J. W. (2000). Nine lives: Adolescent masculinities, the body, and violence. Boulder, CO: Westview Press.

Metzl, J. M. (2010). The protest psychosis: How schizophrenia became a Black disease. Ionia, MI: Beacon Press.

Meyer III, F. (Spring, 2004). The rise and fall of affirmative action. Texas Review of Law & Politics, 8, 437-534.

Moustakas, C. (1975). The touch of loneliness. Englewood Cliffs, NJ. Prentice Hall.

Moustakas, C. (1990). Heuristic research design, methodology and application. London: SAGE.

Nelson, A. (1994). How Could Scientific Facts be Socially Constructed? Studies in the History and Philosophy of Science, 25, 535–547.

Onwuegbuzie, A. J., & Leech, N. L. (2007) A call for qualitative power analyses. Quality & Quantity: International Journal of Methodology, 41, 105-121.

Painter, N. I. (1991). Who Was Lynched? The Nation, 253(16), 577.
Painter, N. I. (2010). The History of White People. New York, NY: W. W. Norton & Company, Inc.

Palmer, C.A. (2002). Passageways: An interpretive history of Black America. Belmont, CA: Wadsworth.

Pennsylvania Department of Health (2013). Office of Health Equity. Black/African American Health Status Overview. Retrieved from file:///C:/ Users/cp8081/ Downloads/AA_11_07_11.pdf

Peterson, R. D., Lauren J., & Krivo, J. H. (2006). The many colors of crime: Inequalities of race, ethnicity, and crime in America. New York, NY: New York Press.

Pettigrew, T. F. (1979). The ultimate attribution error: Extending Allport's cognitive analysis of prejudice. Personality and Social Psychology Bulletin, 5, 461-477.

Philogène, Gina, (1999). From Black to African American: A new social representation. Westport, CT: Praeger.

Pickren, W. E., & Dewsbury, D. A. (2002). Evolving perspectives on the history of psychology. Washington, D.C.: American Psychological Association.

Pitts, M. J. (2008). "The Voting Rights Act and the Era of Maintenance". Alabama Law Review 59, 904-905.

Platek S. M., Krill A. L., & Wilson B. (2009). In-group and out-group membership mediates anterior cingulate activation to social exclusion. Frontiers in Evolutionary Neuroscience, 1. doi:10.3389/neuro.18.001.2009.

Plessey v. Ferguson, 163 U.S. 537 (1896).

Polkinghorne, D. (1995). Narrative configuration in qualitative analysis. Qualitative Studies in Education, 8, 5-23.

Polkinghorne, D. E. (2007). Validity issues in narrative research. Qualitative Inquiry, 13, 471-486.

Reinarman, C., Waldorf. D., Murphy, S. B., & Levine, H. G. (1997). The contingent call of the pipe: Bingeing and addiction among heavy cocaine smokers. In C. Reinarman & H. G. Levine, Crack in America: Demon drugs and social justice (pp. 77-97). Berkeley, CA: University of California Press.

Robertson, J. M., Woodford, J., Lin, C. W., Danos, K. K., & Hurst, M. A. (2001). The (un)emotional male: Physiological, verbal, and written correlates of expressiveness. Journal of Men's Studies, 9, 393.

Rogers, Carl. (1959). A theory of therapy, personality relationships as developed in the client-centered framework. In S. Koch (Ed.),

Psychology: A study of a science. Vol. 3: Formulations of the person and the social context. New York, NY: McGraw Hill.

Rome, D. (2004). Black demons: The media's depiction of the African American male criminal stereotype. Westport, CT: Praeger.

Rosenthal, R., & Jacobsen, L. (1966). Teachers' expectancies: Determinants of pupils' IQ gains. Psychological Reports, 19, 115-118.

Ruggles, D. (2010). A radical Black abolitionist and the underground railroad in New York City. University of North Carolina Press.

Russell-Brown, K. (1998). The color of crime: Racial hoaxes, white fear, Black protectionism, police harassment and other macroaggressions. New York, NY: New York University Press.

Salovoy, P., & Sultor, D. J. (1997). Emotional development and emotional intelligence: Educational implications. New York, NY: Basic Books.

Scheff, T. J. (1966). Being Mentally Ill. 2nd ed. Piscataway, NJ: Aldine Transaction.

Schneider, D. J. (2005). The psychology of stereotyping. New York, NY. Guilford Press.

Schreiber, D. and Iacobini, M. (2012). Huxtables on the brain: An fMRI study of race and norm violation. Political Psychology 33, 314-330.

Schur, E. (1965). Crimes without victims: Deviant behavior and public policy: Abortion, homosexuality, drug addiction. Englewood Cliffs, NJ: Prentice Hall.

Shamir, M., & Travis, J. (2002). Boys don't cry? Rethinking narratives of masculinity and emotion in the U.S. New York, NY: Columbia University Press.

Shelby County v. Holder, 570 U.S. (2013).

Shiraev, E., & Levy, D. (2007). Cross cultural psychology: Critical thinking and contemporary applications (3rd Ed.). Boston, MA: Pearson.

Strauss, A., & Corbin, J. (1998). Basics of qualitative research: Techniques and procedures for developing grounded theory (2nd ed.). Thousand Oaks, CA: Sage.

Sutherland, E. H. (1949). White collar crime. New York, NY: Dryden Press.

T

Talbot, K., & Durheim, K. (2012). The Princeton trilogy revisited: How have racial stereotypes changed in South Africa. South African Journal of Psychology, 42, 476–491.

Tannebaum, F. (1938). Crime and community. Boston, MA: Ginn & Company.

Taylor, S. J., & Bogdan, R. (1998). Introduction to qualitative research methods: A guide and resource. New York, NY: Wiley.

Tower, J., & Arbeitman, M. (2009). The genetics of gender and life span. Journal of Biology, 8(4), 38. doi:10.1186/jbiol141

U

Uniform Crime Report (2012). The Federal Bureau of Investigation. Crime in the U.S. Retrieved from http://www.fbi.gov/about-us/cjis/ucr/crime-in-the-u.s/2012/crime-in-the-u.s.-2012/ tables/43tabledatadecoverviewpdf

Unnger, J. D., & Cullen, F. T. (2012). White perception on whether African American and Hispanics are more prone to violence and support for the death penalty. Journal of Research in Crime and Delinquency, 49, 519–544.

U.S. Bureau of Labor Statistics. (2010). Table A-2. Employment status of the civilian population by race, sex, and age. Retrieved from http://www.bls.gov/news.release/empsit.t02.htm

U. S. Department of Commerce, Census Bureau (2008). Current Population Survey.

U.S. Department of Labor (2014). Bureau of Labor Statistics. Retrieved from http://www.bls.gov/news.release/empsit.t02.htm.

U.S. v. Blewett, 719 F.3d 482 (6th Cir. 2013).

U.S. Sentencing Commission (2014). Fair Sentencing Act Preliminary Crack Retroactivity Data Report. Retrieved from http://www.ussc.gov/sites/default/files/pdf/research-and-publications/federal-sentencing-statistics/

Webster, L., & Mertova, P. (2007). Using narrative as a research method: An introduction to using narrative analysis in learning and teaching. New York, NY: Routledge.

Wellford, C. (1975). Labeling theory and criminology: An assessment. Social Problems, 22, 332-345.

West, C., & Zimmerman, D. H. (1987). Doing gender. Gender and Society, 1, 125-151.

White, K. (2002). An introduction to sociology of health and illness. Thousand Oaks, CA: SAGE.

Wilder, C. (2013). Ebony and Ivy: The troubled history of American universities. New York, NY: Bloomsbury Press.

Wystma, L. A. (1994). Punishment for just us: a constitutional analysis of the crack cocaine sentencing statutes. George Mason Independent Law Review, 3, 474.

Yosso, T. J. (2006). Critical race counterstories along the Chicana/Chicano Educational Pipeline. New York, NY: Routledge.

www.ingramcontent.com/pod-product-compliance
Lightning Source LLC
Chambersburg PA
CBHW072344100426
42738CB00049B/1761

www.ingramcontent.com/pod-product-compliance
Lightning Source LLC
Chambersburg PA
CBHW072344100426
42738CB00049B/1761